# GUINNESS BOOK OF COLLEGE RECORDS & FACTS

**GUINNESS MUSEUMS AROUND THE WORLD**
- **Empire State Building** New York City
- **Ocean Boulevard** Myrtle Beach, S.C.
- **Clifton Hill** Niagara Falls, Canada
- **Parkway** Gatlinburg, Tenn.
- **Lake of the Ozarks** Missouri
- **Fisherman's Wharf** San Francisco
- **Tivoli** Stockholm, Sweden
- **Fuji Safari Park** Gotemba, Japan
- **Linnonmake (Borgbackem)** Helsinki, Finland

# GUINNESS BOOK OF COLLEGE RECORDS & FACTS

By the Editors of Guinness

Peter Cardozo • David A. Boehm • Roberta Morgan
Jim Benagh • Mark Fried • Stephen Topping

Sterling Publishing Co., Inc.   New York

## GUINNESS BOOKS
Guinness Book of Amazing Achievements
Guinness Book of Amazing Animals
Guinness Book of Astounding Feats and Events
Guinness Book of College Records and Facts
Guinness Book of Daring Deeds and Fascinating Facts
Guinness Book of Dazzling Endeavors
Guinness Book of Essential Facts
Guinness Book of Exceptional Experiences
Guinness Book of Extraordinary Exploits
Guinness Book of Phenomenal Happenings
Guinness Book of Sports Records, Winners and Champions
Guinness Book of Sports Spectaculars
Guinness Book of Startling Acts and Facts
Guinness Book of Superstunts and Staggering Statistics
Guinness Book of Surprising Accomplishments
Guinness Book of Women's Sports Records
Guinness Book of World Records
Guinness Book of Young Recordbreakers
Guinness Game Book
Guinness in Spanish and English
According to Guinness

## GUINNESS FAMILY OF BOOKS
Air Facts and Feats
Animal Facts and Feats
Antique Firearms
Antiques
Art Facts and Feats
Astronomy Facts and Feats
Ballet
Bicycling
Boating Facts and Feats
Car Facts and Feats
Darts
English Furniture 1760-1900
Equestrianism
Golf Facts and Feats
Grand Prix Motor Racing
History of Air Warfare
History of Land Warfare
History of Sea Warfare
Motorboating Facts and Feats
Motorcycling
Motorcycling Facts and Feats
Mountains and Mountaineering Facts and Feats
Movie Facts and Feats
Music Facts and Feats
Rail Facts and Feats
Steeplechasing
Tank Facts and Feats
Towers, Bridges and Other Structures
20th Century Fashion
Weather Facts and Feats

Main entry under title:

Guinness book of college records & facts.

1. Universities and colleges—United States—History—Miscellanea.  2. Curiosities and wonders.
I. Guinness book of world records.
LA226.G84      378.73      81-85043
ISBN 0-8069-0230-2      AACR2
ISBN 0-8069-0231-0 (lib. bdg.)

Copyright © 1982 by Sterling Publishing Co., Inc.
Two Park Avenue, New York, N.Y. 10016
Distributed in Canada by Oak Tree Press Ltd.
% Canadian Manda Group, 215 Lakeshore Boulevard East
Toronto, Ontario M5A 3W9
*Manufactured in the United States of America*
*All rights reserved*

# Preface

This book does by no means purport to contain every important fact concerning each one of the thousands of colleges and universities in the United States. It is not a directory designed for students seeking admission into college; it is rather for those who want to be entertained by the more amusing and interesting facts concerning college life, through its initial founding in the new colonies to the massive quasi-city campuses of today.

For those who are thinking of going to college, or who have been through it, or certainly for those who are now attending, this book should provide a great deal of amusement and elucidation. Within its pages you will find out which school is the largest, the most expensive, the smallest, the coldest. You will learn about the highlights in the history of academia, the pranks which have flavored it, and the famous people who have been through it. Sports records, eating records, learning records and even co-ed activities records will be uncovered here.

Your school is probably mentioned in one of these pages. If not, the editors can but apologize, excusing themselves by noting that a thorough treatment of every American college existing today would be like providing all the major facts concerning every large U.S. city—a task that would encompass thousands of pages.

So has the world of college education grown. We hope you will enjoy reading about it, as much as we have enjoyed gathering and researching the records, facts and foibles contained in this book. We would like to thank all the schools who responded to our inquiries for information—without their help, many of the items mentioned here might have been lost to history.

—THE EDITORS

A typical college campus? This idyllic scene is at the University of Kansas in Lawrence.

# I. Odd Bodies

### Preserving the Culture

Located beneath the campus of Oglethorpe College in Atlanta, Georgia, is the Crypt of Civilization, the first successful attempt to bury a record of this culture for any future inhabitants or visitors to the planet Earth. Conceived in 1935 by the college's president, Thornwell Jacobs, the swimming pool-sized crypt was begun in 1938. It was completed and sealed in 1940, and is scheduled to be opened in 8113 A.D. The crypt is filled with writings, newsreels, recordings, and samples from the world of 1940. Included are a quart of beer, a set of Lincoln logs, a Donald Duck doll, an electric toastolater, and a baby's pacifier. Also included is a device designed to teach English to the crypt's finders.

Notre Dame's Lab-For-Germ-Free Life has set in its cornerstone a similar device. It is a copper box containing samples of viruses, vitamins, insects, bacteria and fungi, which were placed there in 1947. It is to be opened in 2147, in order to complete an experiment determining the longevity of the specimens contained therein.

### Unusual Schools

For those who wish to shun the conventional college curriculum, the following schools should provide an interesting alternative:

The Western College of Auctioneering in Billings, Montana, was founded in 1948 and will teach the skills of auctioneering in two weeks for a tuition fee of $350.

The Bartending School of Mixology in Hartford, Connecticut, founded 1947, will teach students the secrets of a good Bloody Mary in seven to ten weeks for the cost of $800.

The United States Brewing Academy, in Mount Vernon, New York, established in 1868, will, in two weeks, for $500, explain why your moonshine may leave something to be desired.

The North Texas Horseshoeing Institute, in Grapevine, Texas, founded in 1966 and running a ten-week course for $750, will teach you just what its name implies.

The College of Comedy, in Elbern, New Jersey, will, in 15 weeks, for $115, teach you how to look and act funny.

## Enhancing Physics

Jearl Walker, a full professor of physics at Ohio's Cleveland State University, doesn't think that his subject has to be boring. He feels that the excitement of physics can be communicated by the way in which it is taught. For instance, when Walker starts his lecture on gravity, he starts with a pratfall. He used to walk on hot coals (before he badly burned his foot) to show how perspiration could provide insulation. And to illustrate the properties of sound, he dresses up in drag as a cheerleader. Every year some 800 undergraduates vie for the 250 seats in Walker's lecture course, even though he is a demanding instructor who fails about five percent of his students.

## 'Round the World

Friends World College has no campus but lots of space. Students attending this school study in 75 different nations, like India, Guatemala, Africa, Japan, and England. They apprentice with artists, social work-

The bells of Alfred University in upstate New York are the oldest set of carillons in the New World. Some were cast as early as 1674.

8 ▪ College Records ▪

No, it's not Albert Einstein as a young man. It's Professor Jearl Walker, who dresses up this way to teach the theory of relativity to his classes at Cleveland State University in Ohio. To accompany his lecture on weight distribution, Prof. Walker lies on a bed of nails with another bed of nails on top of him and has students hit a concrete block on top of him with a sledgehammer. He is not trying to establish a new Guinness world record—he just wants to show it doesn't hurt if you know the principles of physics. Are his courses popular? You can bet on it.

ers, anthropologists and the like, getting first-hand, on-the-job experience. Friends is known as "the Peace Corps of colleges."

### Oldest Bells

Alfred University in Alfred, New York, boasts the oldest set of carillon bells in the Western Hemisphere. The 47 bells are representative of three centuries—18 were cast in 1674, and 14 more were cast in 1737. The remaining bells are of more recent origin.

### UnHistory

One of the more unusual courses offered at the University of Texas at El Paso is taught by Professor Avriam Davidson. It is called *Adventures in UnHistory,* and covers such topics as "The Buttocks of the Queen of Punt," "Who Made the Mermaids?" and "Eunuchs and Unicorns."

Is this the Himalayan mountain kingdom of Bhutan? No, it's the campus of the University of Texas at El Paso, where the architecture was inspired by Bhutanese buildings. The terrain of El Paso is similar, and the wife of the first dean got the idea from an article in the *National Geographic* magazine.

## Trivia Kings

At the University of Wisconsin at Stevens Point there is, through the auspices of the college radio station (WWSP), the largest annual Media Trivia contest in the world. It is a 56-hour contest, involving 500 teams of 8,000 to 10,000 players. It is called *TRIVIA* and is recognized by the United States Trivia Association as the biggest of its type. In 1977, the telephone lines at Stevens Point melted as a result of the number of callers participating in the contest.

## Stretching the Dollars

The University of the South in Tennessee has a Silly Putty Fund, donated by F. Reid Buckley (William F. Buckley's brother). According to college officials, it was named as such because it will stretch, but if it is hit too hard it will break!

## Ring Those Chimes!

Bucknell University in Lewisburg, Pennsylvania, has a set of bells—The Rooke Chapel Chimes—which toll every quarter hour from 7 A.M. to 11 P.M. Bucknell, by the way, is also known for its 1876 graduate, N. Hoffman Moore, the man who devised the white line which runs down the center of all roads.

## Most Unusual Architecture

The University of Texas at El Paso's architectural style was copied directly from the April, 1914, issue of the *National Geographic.* This issue carried an article, lavishly illustrated in sepia-toned photographs, of the hidden Himalayan "dragon kingdom" of Bhutan. The wife of the first dean of UT El Paso (then called the Texas State School of Mines and Metallurgy) discerned that the terrain of Bhutan and that of El Paso were similar and that the buildings of Bhutan—with their battered (sloping) walls, high indented windows, brick-and-tile decorative bands between the windows, and reddish hipped roofs—were somehow a perfect blend with their background. She suggested to her husband that the Mines campus (then being planned) ought to emulate Bhutan. The first Mines buildings (1916) and all which have followed since have hewn to Bhutanese design, the only example of this architecture to be found in the Western Hemisphere.

## College for China

According to a 1970 Gallup Poll, 52% of college-educated respondents thought Communist China should be admitted to the United Nations, compared with 32% of high-school-educated people, and 26% of the people with eight years of schooling or less.

In Houghton, Michigan, the weather is cold enough and the snow and ice plentiful enough for Michigan Tech students to build sculptures like the frozen locomotive (above) and the figures on the opposite page. Some idea of the size of the snow sculptures is shown by the need for scaffolding in the photo on the left.

## Not Just Snowmen

At Michigan Tech, students go beyond snowball-tossing and snowman-building when winter approaches. The school is expert at full ice and snow sculptures, some of which are truly works of art. Scaffolding is used to construct some of the figures, which range from 100-foot-high clowns to full-scale locomotives to carefully carved statues on building fronts made entirely of snow and ice.

## Ivy League Clubs

A cherished tradition at many Ivy League schools is the closed clubs and societies (different from fraternities and sororities) that students so honored are asked to join.

At Harvard, the clubs are: The Porcellian, where members are usually chosen from the "upper-crust" of society; The Fly; and The Delphic. At Yale, you can join St. Anthony Hall, which has a branch at Columbia; The Elizabethan Club, otherwise known as "The Lizzie," whose membership is limited to 40 admittants; The Skull and Bones, Yale's most secret society; or The Scroll and Key. Princeton features The Ivy, which has its own wine cellar; the Cottage; and The Cap and Gown, the only one of Princeton's three clubs to accept women.

## Frat Crazy

The University of Virginia boasts the largest proportion of the student population to be involved in faternity life. A full 40% of all undergrads are in some fraternal organization.

Randolph Hall in Charleston, South Carolina, may look modern but it is one of the oldest college buildings in continuous use since its erection in 1828–29.

### Oldest College Building

Randolph Hall, located at The College of Charleston in South Carolina, and named for the late President Harrison Randolph, is one of the oldest college buildings in continuous use in the United States. The central portion was built in 1828–29.

### Elite Schools

Certain colleges in the country are known for having a large number of students who previously attended prep or private schools. One such place is Hampden-Sydney College in Virginia, where 51% of the students come from private schools. They even publish their own etiquette book, called *To Manners Born, To Manners Bred.* At Hollins College, also in Virginia, 63% come from private schools.

### Wordy Students

A child of five possesses approximately 1500 words in his vocabulary. Upon entrance to a university, the same child has a total vocabulary of 20,000 words, and upon graduation he boasts a total of 60,000 words. However, most people use only 10% to 20% of their total vocabulary store in everyday life.

## Seeing the World

The Babson World Globe, located at Babson College in Wellesley, Massachusetts, is a world-famous item, indeed. The globe weighs 25 tons, is mounted on a 22-inch-diameter, 6-ton hollow shaft representing the axis of the earth, set at an angle of 23.5° from the vertical, and is so devised as to rotate about its axis at speeds ranging from one revolution in four minutes to one revolution in two hours.

The globe is a great steel ball 28 feet in diameter in 20 different colors created in porcelain enamel. Every country in the world is represented, with the capitals and cities with a population of one million or more indicated by stars or circles, respectively. Major mountain ranges, rivers, lakes, islands, island groups and depths of the different oceans are also represented. The total cost of the project was $200,000.

## Two Colleges Share Campuses

St. John's College in Annapolis, Maryland, founded 1696, and Sante Fe College in New Mexico, founded in 1964, share twin campuses and faculty, and the students are granted open transfer privileges back and forth between the two schools.

**The world's largest globe resides on the campus of Babson College in Wellesley, Massachusetts. At a cost of $200,000 the globe shows mountains, rivers, etc., in three dimensions.**

## Spacey School

The University of Arizona at Tucson boasts an 186-inch telescope on its campus. Its Kitts Peak National Observatory has attracted scores of NASA personnel. Arizona telescopes helped to establish the reputation of the school's optical science center. Actually, it was the University of Arizona's scientists who designed the optics for the *Pioneer II* spacecraft.

## Blue-Collar President

Haverford College, in Haverford, Pennsylvania, is known for its former president, Jack Coleman, who took a much-publicized sabbatical in 1973, during which time he worked as a ditch-digger, a garbageman, and a salad-maker. He detailed his experiences in his book, *Blue-Collar Journal*.

## Wellesley Lore

At Wellesley College in Massachusetts, the campus features 550 acres on which lie a nine-hole golf course, squash and tennis courts, soccer, field hockey and lacrosse fields, an Olympic-sized indoor swimming pool, and a beautiful outdoor lake (Lake Waban). Legend at this school has it that the winner of the annual springtime hoop-rolling contest will be the first in her class to marry.

## Mascots

The mascots of Ivy League schools figure heavily in the rituals and games conducted on those campuses. They serve as a symbol of the school both on campus and off. The mascots of the Ivy Leaguers are as follows:

| | |
|---|---|
| Brown | Bear |
| Columbia | Lion |
| Cornell | Big Red (*Indian*) |
| Dartmouth | *Indian* |
| Harvard | *Puritan* (*Crimson*) |
| University of Pennsylvania | *Quaker* |
| Princeton | *Tiger* |
| Yale | *Bulldog* |

## Where Is This School?

Despite its name, Boston College is neither in Boston nor is it a college. It is located in Chestnut Hill, Massachusetts, and is a full-fledged university, with an enrollment of 13,000.

## Frisbee Fun

At Arizona State University at Tempe, 30 students will take a course called *Disc Skills 105* taught by instructor D. William Williams. What does this course teach? Why, Frisbee throwing, of course! The teacher of the unique program explains that to learn this skill properly, students must first understand the principles of aerodynamics, airfoils, Newton's Law, angular momentum, velocity, gyroscope theory, weather, and flight physics.

Courses similar to this one are now being offered at over 40 colleges. A point in favor of the skill—there has never been a known fatality and the total cost for equipment runs about $3!

## About Vassar

☐ On June 19, 1867, the first Vassar commencement was held in the chapel for four graduates.

☐ Vassar's main building was modeled after the Tuilleries Palace in France, which is known today as the Louvre.

☐ In 1878, the first elevator was installed, out of necessity. Vassar women had worn down the stair banisters by using them as slides.

☐ In 1887, Lucy Maynard Solomon '74, became Vassar's first history professor. To pay her salary, students voted to turn down the gas when they left their rooms and gave up eating preserves for a whole week.

☐ The 10 P.M. bedtime rule was abolished in 1900.

☐ Until 1916, Vassar students never saw their grades—only their class standing.

## The Biggest Library Loss

Have you ever kept a book out of the library longer than you were allowed? In 1823, a book on diseases was checked out of the University of Cincinnati's Medical Library. It was finally returned on December 7, 1968 by the borrower's great grandson—only 145 years later. The fine was a hefty $22,646, but the sympathetic library decided not to press collection of the sum.

## Youngest Undergraduate

The youngest undergraduate in U.S. college history was Dr. Merrill Kenneth Wolf (born August 28, 1931) of Cleveland, Ohio. He took his B.A. in music from Yale University in September, 1945, at the tender age of 14.

## Shortest College Career

Want to get through college quickly? That's exactly what Anthony May of Indiana University wanted—and he got his wish. The 18-year-old student became a college senior in 1980 after graduating from high school only seven months before and completing only one semester of higher education. The enterprising young man accomplished this feat by earning the equivalent of 71 credit hours from exams given by the College Entrance Examination Board and his own college department. Anthony claims that he was trying to save his father money by finishing college in record time.

## Gator-Aide

Strange, elongated creatures stroll the campus of the University of Southwestern Louisiana in Lafayette, La. No, they're not basketball players, but rather a dozen alligators who are kept on campus, strolling among the students until they grow large enough to be hazardous, at which time they are shipped to a local game reserve. On March 18, 1976, students at the school further showed their kinship to creatures of the sea by consuming seven-and-a-half tons of boiled crawfish.

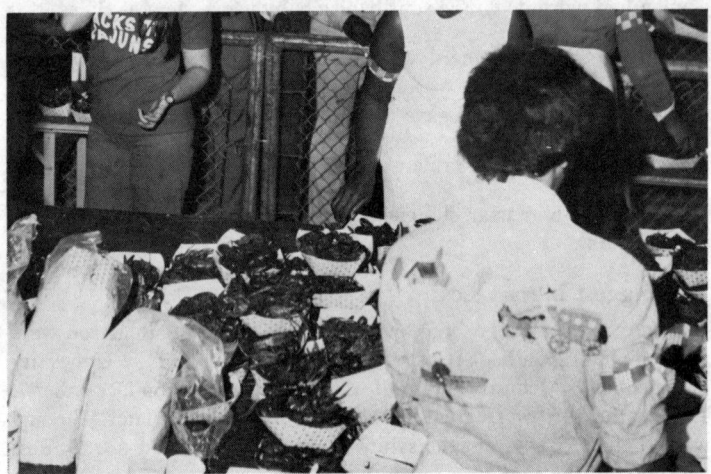

The largest "crawfish boil" in the world is the claim made by the University of Southwestern Louisiana in Lafayette. An estimated 15,000 pounds of crawfish (small lobsters) are boiled on Lagniappe Day, a holiday celebrating the Cajun custom of "something extra." Classes are called off, and games and other entertainment go on throughout the day, culminating in the feast.

Swans and alligators inhabit the bayous and swim around the cypress tree roots in the middle of the campus at the University of Southwestern Louisiana in Lafayette.

- Odd Bodies - 19

## Most Durable Professor

Dr. Joel Hildebrand (born Nov. 16, 1881), Professor Emeritus of Physical Chemistry at the University of California at Berkeley, first became an assistant professor in 1913, and was still conducting active research in 1978.

## Youngest Professor

The U.S. record for youth in professorship is held by Dr. Harvey Friedman, Ph.D. who was appointed Assistant Professor of Mathematics at Stanford University, California in July, 1967. At the time of his appointment, he was 3 months short of being 19 years old.

## Youngest College President

At age 31, only a decade after her own graduation, Ellen Futter became the youngest college president, appointed to head Barnard in May, 1981. In September, 1981, she gave birth to a 5-pound 9-ounce girl—on her 32nd birthday.

The last time a Barnard College head became pregnant, in 1901, she informed the board of trustees and was promptly dismissed.

## Oldest Homecoming Queen

Ms. Rita Reutter, a student at the University of Central Florida in Orlando, boasts that she is the oldest queen to adorn a college homecoming parade. In February, 1977, she sat atop the main float at age 59 years, 4 months. The school would seem to be predisposed to such students, as just the year before, it graduated Vera Williams, at age 76 years, 8 months.

## Like Father, Unlike Son

William Jewell College in Liberty, Missouri, boasts a distinguished member of their Board of Trustees, who served for several years following the school's founding in 1849. The well-remembered college board member was Jesse James' father, who, unlike his outlaw son, was a highly respected man in the community and a minister to boot.

## Learning Behind Bars

Cayuga Community College in Auburn, New York, has, since 1970 been offering 30 courses in subjects ranging from art to marketing. The unusual thing about these courses, however, is the students. They are all inmates of the Auburn Correctional Facility—a maximum security New York State prison. So far, the program has spawned 33 graduates, with degrees in Business Administration and Liberal Arts. The college has recently started construction on the first college library to be built inside a N.Y. prison.

The University of Houston at Clear Lake boasts a similar record—but with a twist. Here, where more maximum security inmates are taught, one professor claims his students possess more tattoos on their bodies than he has ever seen previously.

### Most Industrious Student

The late Ken Tucker (who died one year after graduating) must hold the record for the most ambitious learner. In 1978 Ken had chalked up 400 credit hours at Marshall University in West Virginia in order to receive his B.A. in art. However, his fellow students were quick to point out that he only *needed* 128 credit hours to earn his degree!

**Bundling up is a necessary custom at Iñupiat University of the Arctic in Alaska, which bills itself as the northernmost college in the world.**

### Eskimo Education

Iñupiat University of the Arctic is certainly one of our most unusual schools. Besides being the college located the farthest north in the world, it also features a faculty that for the most part doesn't even have high school degrees. Major programs at this school concentrate on such subjects as Eskimo dancing and parka-making.

### Bass, Anyone?

If you're a bass-fisher, you should check into Indiana State University at Terre Haute, where 10,000 enrollees from ten states take courses sponsored by the school's Bass Fishing Institute.

### Aging Student Body

Concord Theological Seminary in Fort Wayne, Indiana, claims the oldest student body in the U.S., with the average attendee pushing 35.

Seventy-five percent of all students at the school are married, but these facts seem to be no hindrance to success. The school contends that 100 percent of its students have jobs waiting for them after graduation.

## Built Too Large

The football stadium at Bucknell University in Pennsylvania boasts an impressive seating capacity of 14,000. The only problem is that there are only 3,100 students attending the school. Hence, Memorial Stadium has only been filled to capacity once, at its opening ceremonies in 1924.

## Spooky School

As far as interesting collections go, Cornell University at Ithaca, New York, must have one of the most unique and most unusual—to a small, strange segment of the population. Cornell boasts the largest collection of books on witchcraft in the world. Happy brewing!

## Mark Twain Changes Residence

In an effort to get culture closer to their students, Elmira College in New York had the cottage where Mark Twain wrote *Huckleberry Finn* moved from its original location in East Hills, New York, to their own campus in Elmira.

## Gambling School

Since the appearance of legalized casino gambling in Atlantic City, New Jersey, several yeas ago, Atlantic City Community College has offered full-credit courses in blackjack, roulette and casino operation.

## GI Living

Colleges across the nation made some rather unconventional alterations to suit the flood of returning GI's from 1945–50. Suddenly bulging with veterans, their wives and children, colleges struggled to construct portable dorms in the form of Quonset huts, trailers, pre-fabricated houses and hastily converted barracks.

At Michigan State, beds had to be moved on and off the gymnasium floor according to the basketball schedule. At the University of Maine, students moved into converted poultry houses. At U.S.C., two students lived in an automobile for seven months and studied at night under street lamps.

## Co-op House

The first cooperative housing on a college campus, necessitated by the financial demands of the depression years, was organized by a sociology professor at Texas A & M in 1932. Twelve students who were deter-

The Mark Twain Study at Elmira College, New York State, is a replica of a Mississippi steamboat pilot house, similar to the one from which Samuel Clemens (his real name) piloted. It was presented to him in 1874 as a surprise gift from his sister-in-law. Twain wrote some of his classic books here.

mined to stay in college, but who could not afford to live in a dorm, renovated an old "haunted house" near campus and did most of the housework and cooking. By 1933, there were 130 students in ten similar units of co-op housing living at Texas A & M.

### Shoe News

When, in the 1950s, the latest styles for campus wear were no longer launched by the Ivy Leaguers, but instead seemed to emanate from some of the smaller, "provincial" schools across the U.S., Harvard decided to take drastic steps. The Harvard Coop started selling "Dusty Bucks," white shoes that had been specially treated to look ever so slightly worn and just a touch dirty.

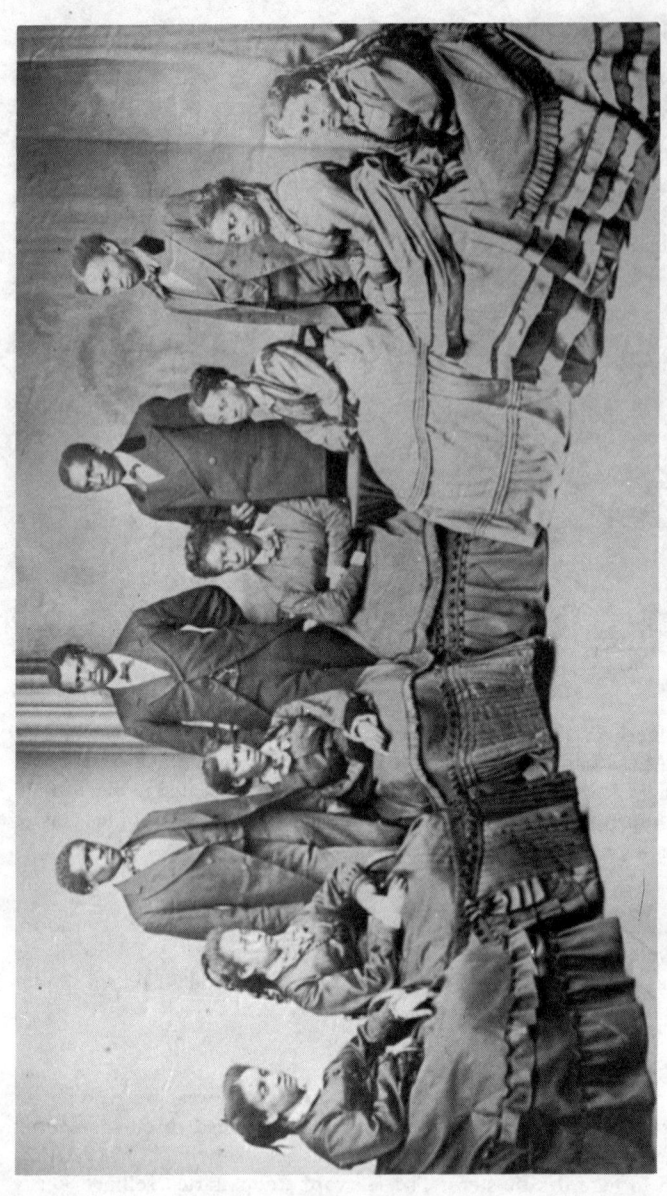

Beginning as early as 1888, Fisk University in Nashville, Tennessee, started students in the entertainment field with their Jubilee Singers. The group has traveled all over, putting on special programs off campus, as well as on.

24 ■ College Records ■

### Singing for Education

The famous Fisk University Jubilee Singers sang to support their school. A Union veteran named George L. White, teaching at the new college, organized the choir out of his newly-freed black students. A fund-raising tour of the country began in 1871. After failing to stir audiences with their classical repertoire, they tried singing a few spirituals—and became an instant hit.

The Fisk singers went on to make a triumphant tour of Europe, and continued their travels in America. Fisk itself began in an abandoned army barracks in Nashville, Tennessee. It was founded in 1866 by Clinton Fisk, a Union general who set out to teach "young men and women irrespective of color." The school became, along with Howard University, one of the nation's most successful black colleges.

### Education Through the Tube

According to *TV Guide* magazine, 60 percent of the PBS (public-supported television) audience have never attended college. This statistic helps to dispel the belief that college-educated people are the only ones who watch the so-called "educational channel."

### Abstract vs. Concrete

Louis Agassiz, famed Swiss naturalist who helped turn Harvard into a university and whose widow helped found Radcliffe, had a statue erected in his honor at Stanford University. When it fell, head-first, during the San Francisco earthquake of 1906, his contemporaries mused: "Agassiz was great in the abstract but not in the concrete."

# II. The Halls of Fame

### The Hall of Fame

The Hall of Fame for Great Americans, which is a feature of the Bronx Community College campus (formerly the Heights Campus of New York University), was proposed in 1899 by Henry M. MacCracken (1840–1918), then chancellor of NYU. It is positioned on a terrace 630 feet long and 25 feet high and includes busts of Lincoln, Washington, Franklin, Harriet Beecher Stowe, Patrick Henry, Walt Whitman, Henry David Thoreau, and Andrew Carnegie. It is now too crowded to accept the busts of any more Great Americans.

### Most Honored Celebrity

The greatest number of honorary college degrees ever granted to one individual—89—is a record held by Herbert Hoover, president of the United States from 1929 to 1933, the years of the Great Depression. Few distinguished scholars can hope to match this feat of honor.

### Celebrity Tidbits

Most colleges can offer up at least one distinguished graduate, who exited through their ivy gates and entered a world of fame in the arts, politic, or sports. Many have left checkered collegiate pasts behind them, or unusual incidents that occurred while they attended school. The following is a cross-section of small facts and tidbits connected with some celebrities' higher education.

F. Scott Fitzgerald was reading the Princeton alumni magazine when he died.

Katharine Hepburn was expelled from Bryn Mawr for smoking a cigarette.

Herbert Hoover was a member of Stanford University's first graduating class (1895).

General Robert E. Lee originated the idea of offering a college course in journalism at Washington University (now Washington and Lee) in 1896.

The original Hall of Fame for Great Americans is in financial trouble. When N.Y.U. sold its Heights campus in 1973 to the City University, the colonnade became the property of the State, but N.Y.U. kept title to the bronze busts. No funds are available now, except for repairs, and the City University pays for these, along with other expenses of the Bronx Community College campus which now surrounds the Hall of Fame.

Woodrow Wilson was president of Princeton before being elected President of the U.S. in 1912.

Charlie McCarthy (Edgar Bergen's dummy) was awarded an honorary degree by Northwestern University. He was dubbed "Master of Innuendo and Snappy Comeback."

Diana Nyad, marathon swimming champ, was expelled from Emory University in Atlanta for parachuting from her dorm window.

General Douglas MacArthur graduated at the top of his West Point class (1903).

Eugene O'Neill was expelled from Princeton for throwing a beer bottle through the college president's window. The president, by the way, was Woodrow Wilson, the only U.S. President ever to possess a Ph.D.

Gore Vidal was born at West Point, where his father was teaching.

Convicted murderess Jean Harris and First Lady Nancy Reagan were classmates and friends at Smith College.

## Infamous and Educated

The infamous "Chicago 7" political activists, of 1960s fame, were all well-educated indeed. They are graduates of the following schools:

> Abbie Hoffman went to Brandeis
> Rennie Davis attended Oberlin
> Jerry Rubin went to the University of Cincinnati
> David Dellinger got his degree from Yale
> Lee Weiner went to the University of Illinois
> John Froines attended the University of California, Berkeley
> Tom Hayden went to the University of Michigan

## Rock Around the Campus

Though the public-at-large may see rock-and-roll stars as the great unwashed and uneducated, this is far from the truth. Rocker Eddie Money attended San Francisco State College, and Pat Benatar went to Stony Brook University.

Becker and Fagin of the group *Steely Dan* went to Bard College, where they started up their very first rock group, with another Bard classmate on drums—Chevy Chase.

The most educated rock group? It's most likely the group *Boston,* whose members amassed their knowledge of electronics from M.I.T.

## Homecoming at Northwestern

When you return to Northwestern University in Evanston, Illinois, as an alumnus you might run into fellow alumni Charlton Heston, McLean Stevenson, Peter Strauss and Robert Conrad, or alumnae Anne-Margaret, Carol Lawrence, Paula Prentiss, Cloris Leachman or Patricia Neal. Amazing how many NW grads went into show business.

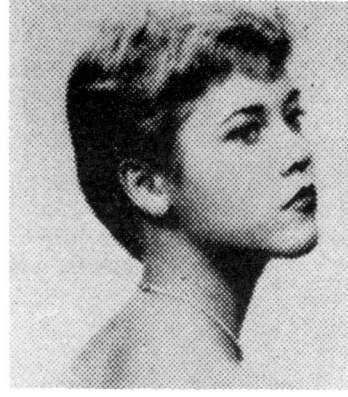

This is the picture of Jane Fonda that appeared in 1955 among the pictures of incoming freshmen (freshwomen?) at Vassar. She only stayed one year—during which she raced through the Victorian-style halls on a high-powered motorcycle.

## Not Graduates

If you are disheartened about never making it into (or through) college, take heart. A university education is not the only ticket to success, as you can see from the following list of noted people who never attended college:

>Ernest Hemingway   H.L. Mencken
>Eleanor Roosevelt  John D. Rockefeller
>Abraham Lincoln    Harry Truman
>Grover Cleveland   J. P. Morgan

## High-Powered Actress

Jane Fonda was said to have been so turned off by her first and only year at Vassar College that she raced through the Victorian-style Main Building (which houses the school's administrative offices) on a high-powered motorcycle.

## Looking at the Heavens

When professor/author/TV personality Carl Sagan (author of *Cosmos* and *The Dragons of Eden*) isn't teaching astronomy or touring the lecture circuit, you can probably find him working with the world's largest radio-radar telescope, operated by Cornell University and located in Puerto Rico.

## Drop-Outs

A large percentage of students drop out of college before they ever receive their degrees. Not that this is an assurance of later failure—as you can see from the cases of three college dropouts—Helen Gurley Brown, innovative leader of *Cosmopolitan* magazine and author of *Sex and the Single Girl;* DeWitt Wallace, founder of *Reader's Digest* magazine; and Carl Bernstein, reporter for the *Washington Post* and co-exposer of the Watergate scandal.

## Motel Success

C. Kemmons Wilson, a high school dropout who built the first Holiday Inn, and who eventually presided over an empire of motels, once recommended an "eighty-hour week" of work to students he was speaking to at the University of Alabama.

## College or Cameras?

Edwin Land, inventor of the Polaroid Land camera, dropped out of Harvard to market his first important development, a plastic that eliminated glare by polarizing light.

## Oldest College Orchestra

The oldest college orchestra in the country was the "Pierian Sodality of 1800 at Harvard," today known as the HRO—the Harvard-Radcliffe Orchestra.

## Dartmouth Flick

If you watch the late, late movie you may catch a 1939 film starring Richard Carlson and Sonja Henie, written by F. Scott Fitzgerald. The name of the flick is *Winter Carnival,* and it was produced at Dartmouth College in Hanover, New Hampshire.

## Syracuse News

Campus disc-jockeys at Syracuse University's FM radio station, WAER, who went on to illustrious careers behind a microphone include American Bandstand host Dick Clark, ABC News correspondent Ted Koppel, sports announcers Marty Glickman, Andy Musser, and Dick Stockton, and WNEW-New York DJ William B. Williams.

Syracuse graduates who succeeded in careers in the entertainment field include Suzanne Pleshette, Peter Falk, Frank Langella, Bob Dishy, Sheldon Leonard, Fred Silverman, and Jerry Stiller.

## Polio Vaccine

Dr. Albert Sabin was a research professor at the University of Cincinnati College of medicine when he perfected an oral polio vaccine. It was cheaper and more stable than Salk's vaccine and provided immunization for life.

At Syracuse University the Hendricks Chapel is the backdrop for sunbathing students when the weather (generally cold) allows it.

### Death Mask

The Hutton Collection at Princeton University boasts the death mask taken from Ludwig van Beethoven, which was cast in 1827, two days after his death. Sir Isaac Newton's death mask, cast in 1727, resides in the same collection.

### Very Literary

The University of Nevada at Reno's literary magazine, called the *Bushfire*, has published works or exclusive interviews with such esteemed figures as Norman Mailer, Joyce Carol Oates, William Stafford, Nicki Giovanni, Richard Armour and others. The magazine has only been in existence since 1973.

### Showtime on Campus

The most successful college-based Broadway musical was *The Student Prince*, and about American college days, *Good News*. The college song most often sung in movies was "Boola Boola," performed by everyone from Nancy Kelly in *Tarzan's Desert Mystery* to Humphrey Bogart in *Sabrina*, to Clark Gable in *Idiot's Delight*. The recorded college song which has sold the most copies is the "Maine Stein Song," which was made popular by Rudy Vallee, the first entertainer to make it a big hit, not just in the college community.

Speaking of entertainers, in the 1920s and 30s, men like Cole Porter and Rodgers and Hart wrote college musicals before they turned pro.

The first television show about college life was Ronald Colman's *Halls of Ivy*.

## Famous "Sisters"

Among the famous alumnae of the "Seven Sisters" colleges are:

| | |
|---|---|
| Katharine Hepburn | Bryn Mawr '28 |
| Helen Keller | Radcliffe '04 |
| Margaret Mead | Barnard '23 |
| Ella T. Grasso | Mount Holyoke '40, A.M. '42 |
| Mary McCarthy (author of the 1954 novel *The Group* which was set at a women's college) | Vassar '33 |

## Vassar Fame

Vassar college sources estimate that the school has so far produced (in terms of alumnae achievements), 1,500 plays, movies, radio scripts, TV showscripts, pamphlets, articles, and books.

## The Princeton Thesis Revelations

Princeton University requires a senior thesis (the length of a small book) before graduation. The works of some famous graduates, though, don't always give clues as to what fields they will pursue in later life. Take the following examples as cases in point. Lisa Halaby ('74), an architecture major, designed a subway station for the corner of 96th Street and Second Avenue in Manhattan. She is now Queen Noor of Jordan. Another career as unforseeable from the senior thesis as Noor's was that of consumer advocate Ralph Nader ('55). His paper was titled "Lebanese Agriculture."

## Pat on the Back

Pat Boone, already a big recording star, entered a program of study at Columbia University leading to a bachelor's degree. Though he is often too modest to recount it, he received straight A's throughout his college career.

## Early Activism

Among the social critics and philosophers who got their start on Ivy League campuses in the first two decades of the 20th century were: e.e. Cummings and Walter Lippmann (who headed the Socialist Club in

Pat Boone, clad in the white buck shoes so popular in the 1950s, graduated *magna cum laude* from Columbia University while he was beginning his singing career in 1958.

1909 at Harvard); F. Scott Fitzgerald and Edmund Wilson at Princeton; and Waldo Frank, Sinclair Lewis, and Archibald MacLeish at Yale.

## Campus Drama

In the early days of Harvard's Hasty Pudding Club, men played both male and female roles in the classic plays presented there. Since the famous drama club's inception in 1844, players have included Henry Cabot Lodge, Justice Oliver Wendell Holmes, J.P. Morgan, Robert E. Sherwood, Jack Lemmon, Archibald Cox, and Alan Jay Lerner.

## Presidential Data

Thomas Jefferson, our third President, was enrolled at the College of William and Mary at age 16.

Our 26th President, Theodore Roosevelt, went to Harvard at age 18.

Warren Harding, the 29th Prez, spent two years at a rural academy known as Ohio Central College—and received his diploma at age 16.

Dwight D. Eisenhower, the 34th President, graduated 61st in his class of 168 at West Point, but he was great in football. He went on to serve as President of Columbia University before becoming President of the United States.

Lyndon Baines Johnson, the 36th President, was the star of the campus at Southwest Texas State Teacher's College in San Marcos, Texas. While in school, he took a part-time job on the janitorial staff.

James Earl Carter, our 39th President, entered Annapolis in 1943 and graduated at age 19 in three years—in the top ten percent of his class. Carter was only 5 ft. 1½ in. tall when he entered college, grew 3 inches taller in his freshman year, and 4 more inches before graduation. His flat feet nearly kept him out of the school. To pass the physical, he rolled his sagging arches over coke bottles each day until they met Navy requirements. He is the only President to have graduated from the Naval Academy.

### T.V. Intellect

The late Allen Ludden, host of the "G.E. College Bowl" and "Password" television game shows of the 1960s, earned the nickname "the happy highbrow" and the "egghead with a rating" because he combined an oustanding college career with the ability to communicate and entertain.

Ludden received both bachelor's and master's degrees in English from the University of Texas in the 1940s, graduating Phi Beta Kappa.

### Harvard's Critic

Statesman Henry Adams said, during the Revolutionary times, that "Harvard College . . . taught little and that little ill."

### Door to Fame

The late Jim Morrison, of the rock group *The Doors,* quit U.C.L.A. two weeks before the end of classes because his student film was rejected and given a "complimentary 'D'." It was at this school that he was given his first chance to perform in public in two campus plays. He attended film school with the famous director, Francis Ford Coppola.

### Theme Song

Among the significant contributions made by early women college graduates, ranks Katherine Lee Bates', who in 1880 wrote "America the Beautiful."

# III. Merry Pranksters

### The Streakers

While in 1920, people had to dance two feet apart during campus dances, 1974 demonstrated the big change in college morals with the advent of "streaking." This term applied to the procedure of running nude through a public place on campus. The University of Florida was one of the first schools to be hit with the streakers, but at other colleges streakers soon followed suit.

At Carleton College in Minnesota, Laura Barton, 18, wearing only a ski mask, sneakers, and red, white and blue socks, streaked to a local theater. Laura lost her boyfriend because of the incident, but remarked later to the Associated Press that "anyone who gets that embarrassed wouldn't be worth dating, anyhow."

### Catsup-Sitting

Rip Howell, a student at the University of Southwestern Louisiana, surprised his peers in December, 1980, by sitting, fully immersed in a keg of catsup, for 17½ hours without a break.

### The Night-Owl School

For students who hate to get up in the morning and love to roam about at night, there's always Triton College in River Grove, Illinois, to consider. Most classes on this campus begin at 11:00 P.M. and run until 4:00 A.M.

### The Fishiest Stunt

The first case of goldfish swallowing was recorded on March 3, 1939, when Lothrop Withington, Jr. of Boston College accepted a bet by swallowing live fish before an audience that included several Boston newspapermen.

Sophomore Irving Clark of the 1939 Harvard class once held the campus record for swallowing more goldfish than any other student in

**How many colleges can boast of having bats on campus? So many bats that the students and children of professors take an annual bat census? Well, that's exactly what happens at St. Cloud State University in Minnesota. This big brown bat was found hiding in a storm sewer.**

history. The enterprising young man downed 24 wriggling, scaly friends. After the feast, he was quoted as saying, "They're kind of bitter, but they go down easy."

By the time Donald Mulcahy of Boston College downed 29 goldfish, the Boston Animal Rescue League ruled the swallowing inhumane and the college outlawed the contest. At Kutztown State Teachers College in Pennsylvania, a student was suspended after swallowing 43 goldfish in 54 minutes, because he was guilty of "conduct unbecoming a student in a professional course."

The last record noted by the *Guinness Book of World Records* was the swallowing of 300 fish by John Parker, a Los Angeles student, in 1974.

## Stop that Pop

In the field of records set by students with the urge to swallow strange articles, John Patrick, a 1939 University of Chicago junior, made a dent in history by eating two-and-a-half phonograph records. The tunes he consumed included "Deep Purple," and "Who's Sorry Now?"

## Batty Students

At St. Cloud State University in Minnesota, the tradition of wintertime bat-collecting has been in full force since 1952. Faculty and students collect all the hibernating bats they can find in local storm sewers; then they examine, band and put them back. Besides providing interesting scientific data on bats, the process also helps the students feel closer to their favorite flying friends, who are quite popular in the area because of the large numbers of mosquitoes they devour in the summer months.

## Shakespearean Monkeys

A Yale University professor decided in 1980 to dispute the long-believed myth that if you could put a bunch of monkeys to work on a typewriter for a extended period of time, they would sooner or later write the complete works of William Shakespeare. The professor determined that "if a trillion monkeys were to type 10 randomly chosen characters a second it would take, on the average, more than a trillion times as long as the universe has been in existence just to produce the sentence: 'To be or not to be, that is the question.' " So much for monkeys replacing students!

## Cafeteria Named for Cannibal

In May, 1968, the student body at the University of Colorado voted to name the new grill room in their cafeteria "The Alferd Packer Grill." Alferd Packer, in case you don't know, was the first man in the U.S. to be convicted of cannibalism, after he consumed his five mining companions during a trip across the Rockies in 1874.

**Was it a mistake to name a campus grill room after a man who consumed his companions when they were stranded in the Rockies in 1874? The University of Colorado students were compassionate when they honored Alferd Packer in this fashion.**

### The Giant Slingshot

Students at William Jewell College in Liberty, Missouri, hold the record for constructing the largest slingshot device ever heard of. The giant weapon was made by stretching surgical elastic between two trees, 15 feet apart. Water balloons were then fired from the device, which projected them as far as 500 yards. There were no casualties, only groups of drenched students.

### The Longest Party

The biggest campus bash on record occurred at San Francisco State College in the spring of 1979. It was there that the campus newspaper staff, calling themselves "The Golden Gaters," carried on the festivities of a single party for three months, two weeks and four days.

### Homecoming Hijinks

Students at Carroll College in Waukesha, Wisconsin, were determined to set new records for homecoming parades. They set one in 1978 by having the shortest parade recorded (less than 100 yards). Still not content, they went on in 1979 to run the whole parade backwards!

### Largest Marching Band

Purdue University claims to have "the largest permanently organized university marching band in the United States," with 380 members and 16 twirlers. Along with its performances at college football games, the "All-American Marching Band" has been designated the official band of the Indianapolis 500 auto race since 1921.

### Passion Puddle

Below Cowles Hall, the original Elmira College building constructed in 1855, is a large pond known as "the puddle." In its early days, when Elmira was a female college, it was traditional for a young lady to escort her beau around the puddle on a sunny afternoon. If by the third circle around, legend has it, the young man had not asked for the lady's hand, she could choose to shove him in.

### Longest Phone Call

The longest continuous phone call ever recorded by the *Guinness Book* before the category was eliminated, lasted for 1,000 hours, from March 12 to April 23, 1975. Students from Western Michigan University in Kalamazoo sat in at the in-house phone in one-hour shifts for 41½ days. The students conducted the call-in to raise money for a medical center for the treatment of burns.

Pets are prohibited on campus at the University of California—Santa Cruz, but this student claims his horse is a means of getting him to class on time from 5 miles away, where he lives. The college agreed. Now the horse needs a parking permit.

## Catch 319

On July 18, 1980, Arden Chapman of Pioneer, Louisiana, who had first set this record while a student at Northeast Louisiana University, caught a grape thrown from a new record distance of 319 feet 8 inches—in his mouth!

## Kidnapped Reptile

On the night of December 10, 1952, a group of students from the University of Texas at El Paso kidnapped a 400-pound, 60-year-old alligator from San Jacinto Plaza in downtown El Paso, put it in the trunk of a Studebaker coupe, drove it to the campus, shinnied up a wall of the geology building and entered through an unlocked window, opened the ground-floor door and carried the alligator to an upper-level office of a distinguished geology professor. The professor opened his door the next morning, walked in, then slowly backed out. His wife, whose office was on the same floor and who taught sociology, happened to stop by. The professor said "Hey, Mary, come see what I've got..."

### Watermelon Toss

Watermelons have been really big at the University of California at San Diego, since 1965. This was the year that the final question on the freshman physics exam concerned the force of impact of a watermelon tossed from the top of one of the campus buildings, Urey Hall. Students testing the answer began a tradition by tossing the melon from the location in question.

In 1976 they set a record for watermelon-tossing: 153 feet 8 inches—from the top of the 8-story lab building. Each year students elect a "watermelon queen," who must carry the largest melon to the top of Urey Hall and toss it onto the cement courtyard below. This event is followed by a watermelon feast.

### Personalized Gift

In 1883, in his junior year, William Randolph Hearst was expelled from Harvard for presenting his professors with a bedpan adorned with each instructor's name and photograph.

### Roughing It

A University of Maryland junior of 1980 found a new way to cut college costs. The 21-year-old architecture major constructed a tent in an area rarely patrolled by campus police, and lived there for several months. He said his weekly bill ran to only $30, which covered his food, cigarettes and drinks. When campus security guards finally discovered him and asked why he wasn't in a dorm, he replied, "I'm waiting for financial aid."

### The Pull

Hope College in Holland, Michigan, has an important tradition, which began in 1897. It is called The Freshman/Sophomore Pull. The tug-of-war takes place across the Black River in Holland. In 1977, The Pull lasted 3 hours 51 minutes before it was declared a tie.

However, it does not qualify as a world record because the international rules forbid bracing the feet. The shortest Rope Pull at Hope lasted 2½ minutes.

A tug-of-war across the Black River is traditional between frosh and sophs at Hope College in Holland, Michigan. One team (sometimes both teams) gets wet before it's over.

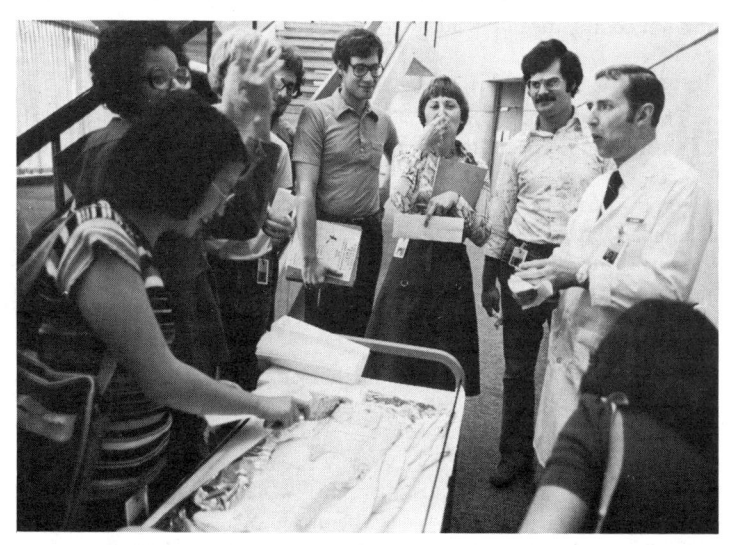

A cadaver-shaped birthday cake? Only medical students would dream up an idea like this. But that is exactly what the students did at the College of Medicine and Dentistry of New Jersey in Newark.

### Eagle Eye

Steven Cloud, a 1979 freshman at Lake Superior State College, Michigan, went out at daybreak on the first day of the hunting season, shot at the first deer sighted (35 miles west of campus), downed it, gutted it, and was back on campus in time for his first class.

### Campus Magazines

The first campus magazines were Princeton's 1830 comic journals *The Thistle* and *The Chameleon*, neither of which survived. The 1870s saw the birth of *The Harvard Lampoon* and *The Yale Record,* which did endure.

### Lampooners

*The Harvard Lampoon,* the premier satire magazine of the colleges, began in 1876, when candidates for membership were instructed to place humorous pieces in a suggestion box. An attempt in 1934 to ban the sale of an issue parodying *Esquire* magazine touched off a protest riot involving 2,000 students. The *Lampoon* in question, which included a drawing of a nude woman, captioned: "What the well-dressed bride will wear," was an immediate sell-out.

The 1966 *Lampoon* parody of *Playboy* magazine sold more than ½ million copies, including 90,000 overseas.

### Jesters

The *Columbia Jester,* first published on April Fool's Day, 1901, boasts of a list of famous editors that included artist Rockwell Kent '04, musical comedy writer Howard Dietz '17, publisher Bennett Cerf '20, writer Herman Wouk '34, cubist-artist Ad Reinhardt '35, monk-author Thomas Merton '38, and author Gerald Green '42.

During the 20s and 30s when *Jester* was in its heyday, it was sold on newsstands for a quarter, even off campus, where it competed with *College Humor,* the national monthly that reached a peak circulation of 800,000.

When a *New Yorker* artist in 1931 helped himself too obviously to a *Jester* idea, the Columbia magazine published the two cartoons side by side in their next issue.

About the same time that *Jester* was supreme on the Columbia campus, other colleges had their star writers and artists—Robert Benchley and George Santayana (before him) on the *Harvard Lampoon,* James Thurber on the *Ohio State Sundial,* S. J. Perelman of the *Brown Jug* and Art Buchwald of the *USC Wampus.*

"You can be a total jackass when you're 19 years old, and still

> **JESTER**
>
> ### The Blue Pencil
> How a Spec nite-ed would condense the Gettysburg Address for a crowded Friday edition.
>
> Lincoln's Gettysburg ~~Address~~ Pa.,
>
> [ ~~Fourscore and seven~~ 87 years ago our fathers brought forth ~~on this continent~~, a new nation, conceived in liberty and ~~dedicated to the proposition~~ *stating* that all men are created equal. [Now we are ~~engaged in a great civil~~ *at* war, testing whether that nation ~~or any nation so conceived or so dedicated~~, can long endure. We are met on a ~~great~~ battlefield of the ~~war~~. We ~~have~~ come to dedicate a ~~portion~~ *part* of that field, as a ~~final~~ resting place ~~of those who~~ *of the men who died here.* ~~gave their lives that that nation might live. It is altogether fitting and proper that we should do this.~~ (Edit Bull) [But ~~in a larger sense~~ /we *stet* cannot dedicate, ~~we cannot~~ consecrate, ~~we cannot~~ hallow this ground. The ~~brave~~ men, ~~living and dead~~, who struggled here ~~have~~ dedicated it ~~far~~ above our ~~poor~~ power to add or detract. The world will ~~little~~ *not* note, ~~nor long remember~~ what we say here, but it can never forget ~~what they did here~~ *their work*. ~~It is for us the~~ living, *should* ~~rather, to~~ be dedicated ~~here~~ to the ~~unfinished~~ work which they who fought here have ~~thus far so nobly~~ advanced. ~~It is rather~~ ~~for us to be here~~ *We should* dedicated to the ~~great~~ task remaining ~~before us~~— *become more devoted to* that from these ~~honored~~ dead we ~~take increased devotion for~~ that cause for which they ~~gave the last full measure of devotion. That~~ *died*. We here ~~highly~~ resolve that the ~~se~~ dead's *honor* ~~shall not have died in vain~~ ~~that~~ *stet* this nation, ~~under God, shall have/a~~ new birth of freedom, and ~~that~~ the government ~~of the people, by the people, and for the people~~, shall not perish, ~~from the earth~~.

**The "Columbia Jester" in 1921 ran this edited version of the Gettysburg Address.**

amount to something later on." These profound words came from *Columbia College Today.*

## Top Banana

On April 26, 1980, the Alpha Phi Omega fraternity of Texas A & M University put together the biggest banana split on record—it was one mile 575 yards long (7,005 feet). The split was constructed with 11,400

Why these long fingernails? Are they a record? Avis Shambes, 21 years old at the time, a student at Chicago State University, was prompted to grow these (maximum 3 inches to the tip) out of curiosity. She has fast-growing nails and merely wanted to see how long they could grow without breaking.

bananas, 1,500 gallons of ice cream, 380 gallons of topping, and 170 pounds of nuts.

### Republican Prank

In 1930, two editors at the *Cornell Sun* made national news when they sent letters to Republican leaders throughout the country, inviting them to a dinner commemorating the sesquicentennial of "Hugo N. Frye, founder of the Republican Party in New York State."

After the Vice President of the United States and several cabinet members telegraphed their praise for the students' worthy gesture, the editors revealed, between snickers, the phonetic resemblance between the fictional Mr. Hugo N. Frye and "You Go and Fry."

### Future Veterans

Students at Princeton in 1936 decided to establish a group called the "Veterans of Future Wars" for the purpose of "collecting their bonus in advance." Their salute consisted of a "hand outstretched, palm up, expectant." Membership in this mock-group spread throughout the undergraduate population of the nation, despite avid protests from the American Legion.

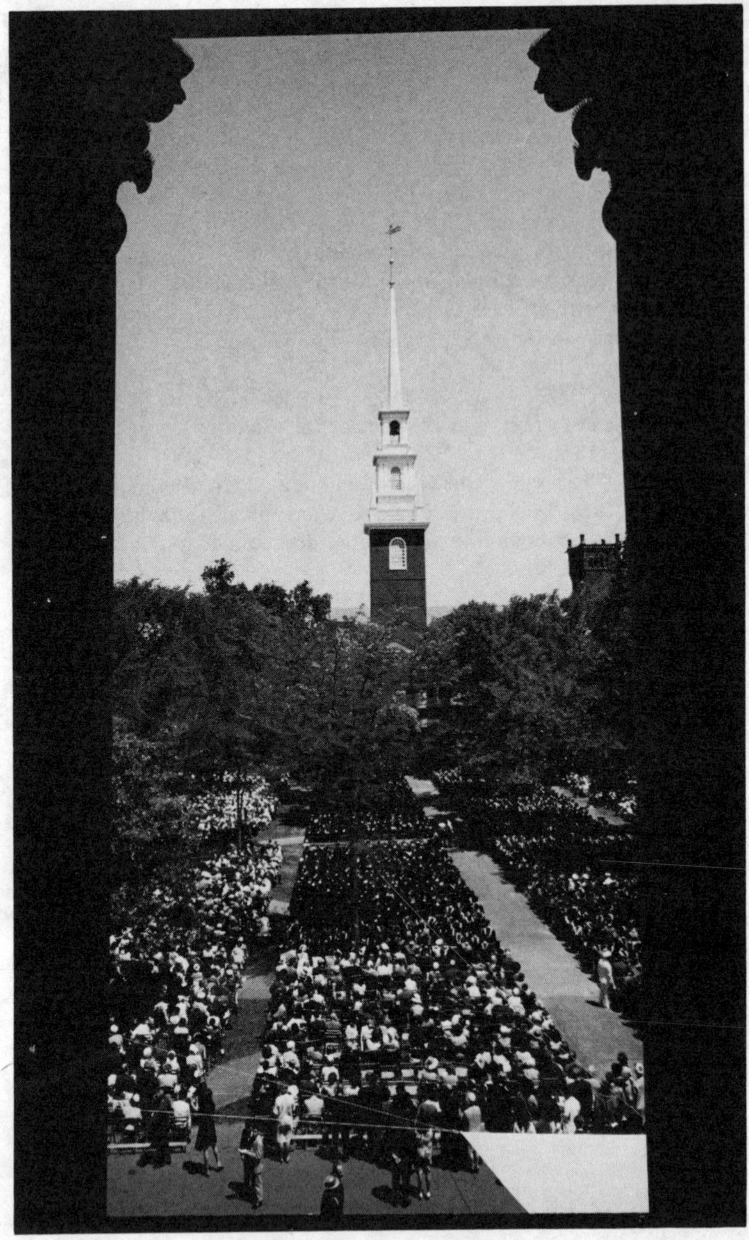

# IV. Size and Stature

## Study Time

The average student in the United States is now estimated to spend about 16,000 hours studying before his entrance into college, and about 6,000 more hours of study while attending college.

## The Progression of College Education

The following table will give you some idea as to how colleges have grown and changed over the years.

|  | 1869-70 | 1978-9 |
|---|---|---|
| Total # of colleges & univ. | 563 | 3,134 |
| Total Faculty | 5,553 | 1,090,000 |
| men | 4,887 | 740,000 |
| women | 666 | 350,000 |
| Total Students | 52,286 | 11,260,092 |
| men | 41,160 | 5,640,998 |
| women | 11,126 | 5,619,094 |
| Masters Degrees | 0 | 311,620 |
| Ph.D. Degrees | 1 man | 23,658 men |
|  | 0 women | 8,473 women |

**(Opposite page)** Commencement exercises at Harvard take place on the campus between the Memorial Church and the Widener, the undergraduate library from which this photo was taken.

(All photos from "Cheerleading and Songleading" by Barbara Egbert)

48 ▪ College Records ▪

Top 20 Cheerleaders

The top 20 cheerleading squads in the nation, according to the International Cheerleading Founding Association in cooperation with the National Collegiate Athletic Association (NCAA), are as follows:
1. Penn State University
2. United States Military Academy
3. Auburn University
4. University of Southern California
5. University of Kansas
6. University of Notre Dame
7. Indiana State University
8. University of Illinois
9. University of California, Los Angeles
10. University of Pittsburgh
11. Ohio State University
12. Marquette University
13. Wake Forest University
14. University of Oregon
15. University of Arizona
16. University of Michigan
17. University of Maryland
18. University of Missouri
19. Brigham Young University
20. University of Iowa

Cheerleading is big business at many colleges in the Far West, Southwest and Midwest in particular. These pictures show the variety of activities that involve cheerleaders.

## Biggest Drum

For many years, both the University of Texas and Purdue University have claimed to have the world's largest drum, at least for a marching band. According to the Purdue press guide, "The big boomer billed by the Purdue All-American Marching Band is the world's largest bass drum. Measurements are classified information." The drum, which was put in service in 1921, reportedly is over 10 feet high. The Texas press guide also lists its bass drum, "Big Bertha," as the world's largest, and gives its measurements as 8 feet in diameter, 54 inches wide and weighing 500 pounds. It takes four bandsmen to carry "Big Bertha." Because of Purdue's secretiveness, the controversy may never be resolved, especially because Purdue claims that Texas never showed at a band gathering in Kansas City, Missouri, in 1963. "So we say we won by forfeit," says a Purdue band director.

## Most Famous Baton Twirling Position

Probably Purdue's Golden Girl, dressed in gold sequins and usually of blond hair, is most famous because of the enormous number of tryouts for the position and constant exposure on national television.

## Most Famous Bandsman's Position

This is probably the person selected annually to dot the "i" when Ohio State's prestigious and nationally known band unravels into "Script Ohio."

## A Small Country

The State University of New York (SUNY), with its 72 educational institutions, has an annual budget that could be used to completely run the governments of Syria, the Philippines, or Trinidad and Tobago.

## Largest Engineering School

Rensselaer Polytechnic Institute in Troy, New York, claims the largest undergraduate enrollment in engineering (2,650 out of a total enrollment of 4,195) of any independent university in the country.

## Largest Radio Station

WKCR-AM and WKCR-FM, Columbia University's radio stations, are the largest collegiate stations in the country.

## Graduate-Oriented

At the University of Chicago, an astonishing 75% of all undergraduates go forward in their education to attend either a graduate or professional school.

What was once ranked as the "world's largest drum" by Guinness is now only the largest college drum. Over 10 feet high, "Big Bertha" of the University of Texas Longhorn Band was made in Elkhart, Indiana, near Purdue University which contests the record. Today's record, however, is held by the Disneyland Big Bass Drum which is 10 feet 6 inches in diameter and weighs 450 lbs.

### Herpes Research

The largest center in the country devoted to the study of the Herpes virus is located at the University of Washington in Seattle.

## Jewish School

Yeshiva University, located in New York City, founded in 1806, is America's oldest and largest university under Jewish auspices.

## Mormon Education

Brigham Young University in Provo, Utah, the school supported by the Mormon (Latter-Day Saints) Church, sponsors a Young Ambassadors European Tour each year, where students go abroad on missionary work for the faith. In 1978 the tour attracted a live, radio and TV audience of about 200 million people. Students at the school, like all Mormons, voluntarily refuse to smoke, drink alcoholic beverages or even imbibe tea or coffee. The latter two beverages are not even served in the cafeteria.

## Most Schools in One Small Town

Carleton College in Northfield, Minnesota, is one of two colleges in this small town. The other is called St. Olaf's. This means that Northfield is one of the only towns in America with more colleges than movie theaters!

## Library, Anyone?

Which population of college students has access to the largest library collection in the U.S.A.? Well, although Harvard's library is the largest of any school's, the answer would technically be the students of George Washington University and the other colleges in Washington, D.C. A brief stroll leads scholars there to the Library of Congress.

## Democratic Ivy

Though Ivy League colleges tend to have a large percentage of students who hail from private schools, they still have many scholarships and part-time working students. Cornell has the highest public school enrollment of any Ivy League college.

## Enrollment Figures

From October 1974 to October 1978, college enrollment increased from 9.9 million to 11.1 million, or about 13%. The largest percentage gains were for blacks and other minorities; people 35 years and older; women; and part-time students.

There were more women enrolled than men in the age group under 20; more men than women in the age group of 20 to 29; from age 30 to 34 the sexes were divided almost equally; and there were many more women than men enrolled in the age group of 35 or older.

## The Ten Universities Which Lead in Expenditures for Research

| | (*In Millions*) |
|---|---|
| University of Wisconsin (Madison) | $ 93 |
| Stanford University | 82 |
| Massachusetts Institute of Technology | 78 |
| Columbia University | 76 |
| Univ. of California (San Diego) | 70 |
| Harvard | 69 |
| Univ. of California (Los Angeles) | 67 |
| Univ. of Washington | 65 |
| Univ. of California (Berkeley) | 64 |
| Univ. of Minnesota (Minneapolis–St. Paul) | 62 |
| Total Expended in Research | $726 million |

## Largest Endowments

The schools having the largest endowments are as follows:

| | |
|---|---|
| Harvard | $1,209,858,000 |
| University of Texas at Austin | 1,091,240,000 |
| Yale University | 544,972,000 |
| Stanford University | 516,234,000 |
| Princeton University | 431,845,000 |

## Revenue

Colleges receive $47,034,032,000 in revenue, but only $9,855,270,000 comes from student tuition. To run the country's colleges, the additional money must be obtained from government grants, foundation and private grants, alumni contributions, and other sales and services.

## State Concentration

Nearly ⅓ of all U.S. colleges and universities are located in five states:

New York has 286
California has 262
Pennsylvania has 178
Illinois has 154
Texas has 147

New York State alone accounts for more than 9% of all institutions of higher learning in the country.

## Higher Higher Education

The University of Wisconsin has 8,145 Ph.D and Ed.D students—more than any other school in the nation.

Not only is Trinity College in Hartford, Connecticut, one of the oldest (founded in 1823), but it is also the most advanced in catering to physically handicapped students through a system of ramps, stair lifts, etc.

## Trinity College Cares

Trinity College, located in the south end of Hartford, Connecticut, was founded in 1823 by Protestant Episcopal churchmen. The unique design of the campus (besides being highlighted by authentic Gothic structures), makes the school 99% accessible to students with physical handicaps. This is done through a system of ramps, elevators, stair lifts, lowered drinking fountains and telephones, and specially-equipped rest rooms.

## The Most Students

| | |
|---|---|
| Univ. of Minnesota (Minn.-St. Paul) | 62,792 |
| Ohio State Univ. | 51,436 |
| Michigan State Univ. | 46,567 |
| Univ. of Texas at Austin | 43,095 |
| Miami-Dade Community College (Florida) | 39,562 |
| Univ. of Wisconsin at Madison | 39,430 |
| Northeastern Univ. (Mass.) | 37,431 |
| Arizona State Univ. | 37,122 |
| Univ. of Maryland (College Park) | 36,905 |
| Univ. of Michigan (Ann Arbor) | 36,577 |

America. (The State University of New York with 344,000 students is dispersed over various campuses.)

## Total Expenditure

If you want to hear a really impressive figure concerning the outlay of money, try this one. In 1978, American universities spent $45,970,790,-000 on research, construction and various expenses.

Toccoa

## A Large Campus Shower

Toccoa Falls College in Georgia is the only school in the United States to own its own waterfall. The Toccoa Falls are actually 186 feet high—which, by the way, is 19 feet higher than Niagara Falls.

Harvard was originally to be called Newtowne (1636), then Cambridge, and finally in 1638 changed to honor John Harvard who died in that year, leaving half of his estate including his library to the new college. His statue is in the hub of the campus.

58 ■ College Records ■

# V. Great Events

## The First American College

In order to stop colonial ministers from becoming illiterate, plans were begun in 1636 to open an institution of higher learning, similar to the ones the early settlers remembered from the old country. To the rescue came the son of a Cockney butcher and a 1635 Cambridge graduate himself, John Harvard. A man who obviously understood how education could improve one's life and social standing, Harvard left half of his estate (£ 780) and 300 books to the new college, which was first named Newtowne College, enabling it to open in 1636 and name itself in his honor. At the time, people hoped Harvard would bring "new life to the surrounding plantations." Harvard did, however, gain a bad reputation with the traditional clergy who first supported it. Many members of its student body and its first president were opposed to infant baptism, which people of the period felt was "one step away from atheism."

## The First Female Applicant

Lucinda Foote, aged 12, was examined by the gentlemen in charge of admissions to Yale University in 1783, and was found to be "fully qualified, except in regard to sex, to be received as a pupil of the Freshman class." Women were then thought to be far inferior intellectually to men, and it was not until 1969 that Yale admitted its first full class of women (although Yale Drama School had been admitting women several years earlier). Lucinda, no doubt, went on to become a dutiful wife skilled in piano playing and home crafts, which was just what was expected of her.

## Odd Endowments

During the American Revolution, there were nine colleges in the country. How did they support themselves? Besides collecting tuition costs, Harvard received the income from the Charlestown ferry tolls; Yale was awarded the take from various privateering and pirating operations; and William and Mary was assisted by Virginia's new taxes on tobacco.

Matthew Vassar, founder in 1865 of the college bearing his name, was a brewer in Poughkeepsie, New York, and had intentions of founding a hospital, before he was persuaded to help educate young women.

## The First Colleges for Women

The question of what was the first women's college is debated by many sources, some of which continue to claim it was Vassar. To set the record straight, Oberlin College was organized in 1833 and accepted four women at college level in 1837 (for a special "Ladies Course") and later accepted women into the regular course program in 1853. Georgia Female College, opened in 1836, is said to be the first to grant degrees. Mount Holyoke Female Seminary opened in 1837, and was chartered as a full-fledged college in 1888.

Elmira College was chartered in 1852. The first state university to accept women was Iowa State, in 1856. Vassar College was opened by Matthew Vassar, a Poughkeepsie brewer, in 1865; Smith and Wellesley began teaching in 1875; Bryn Mawr in 1885; and Barnard in 1889. Radcliffe opened its doors in 1879 and was chartered in 1894.

Vassar president John Howard Raymond in an 1870 letter asked about education for women: "Has she the strength of brain enough to receive it? . . . Will it not destroy feminine grace and delicacy? . . . Will it not break down her physical health?"

## The First Medical School for Women

The Medical College of Pennsylvania in Philadelphia can lay claim to being the first school open to the training of both male and female physicians. It was founded in 1850 and named The Female College of Pennsylvania; in 1867 its name was changed to the Woman's Medical College of Pennsylvania; and in 1970 the title was changed again to its present name. After many years of struggle, the college did its part in getting women recognition by the communities-at-large for their medical skills.

## First Alumnae Association

The first college alumnae association was founded at Wesleyan College in July of 1859. According to the American Alumni Association, although MacMurray College of Jacksonville, Illinois, organized its alumnae two years earlier, it was not a degree-granting institution at that time.

## Most Tragic Campus Demonstration

As any self-respecting historian knows, the late 60s and early 70s saw the rise of political consciousness on U.S. campuses and ensuing mass demonstrations. The worst tragedy to occur during this period was at Kent State University in Ohio, a school previously known mainly for being the birthplace of professional tree surgery. On May 4, 1970, however, Ohio National Guardsmen opened fire on a group of students protesting U.S. intervention in Cambodia. Four students fell dead on campus, and the incident became a rallying point for campus demonstrations around the nation.

Founder of the Columbia School of Journalism in New York City was Joseph Pulitzer, an immigrant from Hungary, who rose to become a lawyer and publisher. The journalism school, through committees, awards the Pulitzer prizes.

## A Big Prize

In May, 1917, the trustees of Columbia University, New York City, handed out the first Pulitzer Prizes, established under a bequest of $1,000,000 by Joseph Pulitzer (1847-1911), publisher of the *New York World* and the *St. Louis Post-Dispatch.* These annual awards were given in recognition for excellence in the fields of journalism, letters and music. Today, the prize is one of the greatest honors an artist or scholar can hope to receive.

## Carpets and Technology

Erastus B. Bigelow of West Boylston, Mass., began construction of the first power loom for the manufacture of Brussels and Wilton carpets in 1845. He went on to establish the Bigelow Carpet Mills, and one thing more—with his expertise and his fortune he helped found the Massachusetts Institute of Technology, known fondly and reverently across the country as M.I.T.

## Going Co-Ed

The first male university (not state-supported) to admit women to its halls was Cornell University, which took the giant step in the year 1870.

## Bartering Education

Institutions of higher learning actually had to resort to the barter system to stay afloat during the Depression years. In the early 1930s,

Carthage College in Illinois accepted coal instead of money for the tuition of a coalminer's daughter. At the University of North Dakota, payment in the form of farm produce was commonplace.

## Have a Drink

The consumption of alcoholic beverages has always been somewhat of a tradition in American colleges. In the 18th century, student canteens were called "butteries" (as in England) and alcohol was usually served there. In 1734, however, Harvard passed a regulation stipulating that no resident of the college must be found drinking distilled spirits in public or in private. The drinking of wine and beer was not discouraged, and continued to be served in the school cafeterias.

## Early Agitators

In 1934, because of pacifist and other radical demonstrations, C.C.N.Y. was sometimes referred to as "The Little Red Schoolhouse." Within just 30 years, most campuses became the scenes of large demonstrations, and C.C.N.Y. no longer had the notoriety for such events that Columbia, Berkeley or Kent State did.

## Fraternity Facts

The oldest Greek letter fraternity in this country was Phi Beta Kappa, founded on December 6, 1776 at the College of William and Mary. Since it was later turned into an honor society, history notes that the oldest general (or social) fraternity in continuing existence is Kappa Alpha Society, founded in 1825 at Union College, Schenectady, New York.

The largest fraternity is Sigma Alpha Epsilon, with 181,900 initiates, located at the University of Alabama and founded on March 9, 1856.

The fraternity with the most active campus chapters is Tau Kappa Epsilon, which boasts 272 individual campus locations.

## First Agricultural School

The pioneer institution of state agricultural colleges of the West and Mid-West was the University of Michigan, chartered at Lansing in 1855. Here, the principle of mass, democratic higher education got its first push.

## The Elective System

Harvard's vital president, Charles William Eliot, who reigned for 40 years starting in 1869, initiated the concept of an elective system of education, where students could choose for themselves all but a few courses in their program of study.

## Masters' Degrees

Up until 1868 the master's degree was an honorary award granted to graduates who had made some important accomplishments in their lifetimes. By 1869, colleges across the nation made it an earned degree, and began to structure two- and three-year programs leading to an M.A.

## Rising Costs

Incredible as it may seem, tuition costs at the University of Georgia in 1867 were $120 per year. With room and board included, costs should reach over $15,000 per year by the year 1990! (Room and board, by the way, ran you an extra $60 in 1867!)

## About Harvard

☐ The resignation of a Harvard president in 1773 was caused by the impregnation by him of one of his house servants. The secret was revealed two decades later, by the publication of a Yale man's diary.

☐ John Langdon Sibley, an 1825 Harvard graduate, decided to write a biography of every Harvard student since the school's inception in 1636. By the time he died in 1886, he had managed to reach the class of 1689.

☐ Up until 1700, Harvard graduated only 543 students—an average of eight per year—half of whom became clergymen. Boys entered at 13 or 14, and the sole requirement for an A.B. degree was the ability to translate the Old and New Testaments from English into passable Latin.

☐ Dr. John W. Welter (class of 1811) was hanged in 1850 for murdering Dr. George Parkman (class of 1809), while both men were on the faculty of Harvard Medical School.

☐ Harvard had its beginnings on one-and-a-half acres of Cambridge farmland. The school now owns over 150 acres, worth (with the price of the buildings included) over $500 million.

☐ In 1886, "Godless" Harvard became the first major American university to do away with compulsory chapel. Even though many critics saw Harvard as a haven for atheists, the school was known by others as "The Seminary" as late as 1834.

☐ The first Harvard summer school was held on an island in Buzzard's Bay in 1870, conducted by two professors of botany. Shortly afterwards, Harvard decided to give up the island, and it became a leper colony.

☐ In 1869, Harvard's endowment was $2.5 million; in 1909 it was $22.5 million; in 1933, $126 million; through the 1960s it was over $360 million; and today it stands at over a billion dollars.

☐ John Harvard, the founder of the school, was the son of an English butcher who died in the 1625 plague. John came to the United States in 1637 to serve as a Presbyterian minister. He died of TB in 1638 and willed his library and £800 to the new college, which was renamed for him.

Of the 400 books Harvard received from its benefactor in 1642, all but one was lost on January 24, 1764 in a massive fire. The book that escaped was John Downame's folio, *Christian Warfare Against the Devill, World, and Flesh*. The book was out of the library with a student who had forgotten to return it.

☐ Harvard's library, the largest of any school's, has 9,913,992 volumes. It ranks third, behind The Library of Congress and The New York Public Library, as the largest of its kind in the nation. The library boasts the possession of the original manuscript of *Look Homeward, Angel*, 16 first editions of *Paradise Lost* and more Keats' manuscripts than all the libraries in the world put together.

☐ The Harvard band was not formed until 1910. Before then, marching at halftime during football games was provided by R.O.T.C. men, with music supplied by banjo and mandolin players.

☐ George Washington received an honorary Harvard degree on April 3, 1776.

☐ The editor of the *Harvard Crimson* in 1904 was Franklin Delano Roosevelt.

☐ As late as 1786, Harvard men were forced to wear elaborate uniforms, different for each year of attendance. It was a serious offense to be caught outside of one's room without wearing the uniform and it being in relatively good shape.

☐ Harvard hired its first Oriental faculty member, for a commercial language course, in 1879. The poor professor succumbed to Western weather in 1882, causing Harvard to get so discouraged it didn't hire another Oriental until 1921.

☐ In 1879, Radcliffe was founded as the Society for Collegiate Instruction of Women. In 1894, it was re-named Radcliffe College to honor the Englishwoman Lady Anne Radcliffe, an early benefactress of Harvard. The schools linked class space (making Harvard essentially co-educational), in 1943, and Radcliffe girls began receiving Harvard degrees in 1963.

Among the first college bookstores was Harvard's, of which this is the modern descendant. Young John Bartlett at age 16 got a job there in 1836, read almost every book in it in the next 13 years, and saved enough money to buy the store and self-publish his now-famous Book of Familiar Quotations. The Harvard bookstore is now a "Coop" (co-op).

## Beanie Fun

Harvard freshmen around the turn of the century were all required to wear beanies as a symbol of subordination to upperclassmen. But, in all fairness, any frosh who could reach the top of a greased flagpole would win himself the privilege of removing his beanie. This beanie-wearing custom continued at many colleges throughout the country well into the 1960s, and the punishments inflicted by some fraternity houses on freshmen caught without their head-coverings were quite severe.

## An Erring President

Clark Kerr, President of the University of California at Berkeley, was certainly no clairvoyant or fortune-teller. He was quoted as saying in 1959 about the student generation of the 1960s: "I can just see . . . that they are not going to press any grievances . . . they are going to do their jobs, they are going to be easy to handle." Sorry, Clark.

## Sitting In

The first student sit-in took place in Greensboro, North Carolina on February 1, 1960. Four black freshmen at the North Carolina Agricultural and Technical College refused to leave a segregated Woolworth's lunch counter until they were served.

## College Cruisers

In 1920, Studebaker stopped making horsedrawn wagons, and the automobile began to be seen regularly on college campuses. But after numerous accidents, in which many students lost their lives, a large number of colleges decided to ban the use of the car indefinitely.

## High and Dry

In 1920, Stanford University banned the drinking of liquor from any quarter of its college campus, after one intoxicated student stumbled into the wrong fraternity house and was shot and wounded, having been mistaken for a burglar.

## Smoke, Anyone?

In response to a ban on smoking in the 1920s, Wellesley College girls went to the town line "to sit on a stone wall in large numbers" and smoke in protest. This event led to the creation of a "smoking room" in 1928. Bryn Mawr permitted smoking by 1925, and Vassar followed suit at the end of the decade.

## College Fines

At Harvard, in 1800, a student would be fined one penny for being late to prayers. The highest fine paid in that year was the sum of fifty shillings (about $12) for "tarrying out of town one month without leave."

## Religion and Colleges

Many early American colleges were established because of religious differences. It is said that the grim preacher Cotton Mather was the one who convinced Elihu Yale to leave his money to the school that was to be named after him, rather than to the god-forsaking Harvard.

A more radical faction of Presbyterians founded Princeton in 1746, which was first chartered as the College of New Jersey.

Enthusiastic Congregationalists backed Eleazar Wheelock when he decided to convert his Indian school into Dartmouth College. Baptists needed a place of their own, and so proceeded to found the College of Rhode Island (later known as Brown University). The Dutch Reformed Church started a New Jersey-based school called Queens, which in 1825 became Rutgers, after Henry Rutgers—a New York merchant who donated $5,000 to its construction.

Episcopalians went on to found King's College (later Columbia College and University), supported by King George II (£ 400), who had hoped the school would "guard against total Ignorance." Alexander Hamilton was a student at King's College (1773–76), and later a building at Columbia College was named for him.

## The Largest Student Riot

The Berkeley Student Revolt, which began on September 14, 1964 and continued through the entire fall semester, is considered to be the first major scale student protest, as well as the first large protest using civil disobedience as a strategy. The confrontation began when the Dean of Students outlawed the solicitation of funds for all off-campus political action groups.

Throughout the early 1960s, Berkeley boasted the largest undergraduate student body of any single institution in the country.

## A Matter of Taste

Princeton's senior class of 1935, in a dramatic example of the effects of popular culture, chose Noel Coward over William Shakespeare as the supreme dramatist, and magazine artist McClelland Barclay over Rembrandt as the greatest painter of all time.

## The Great Unwashed

During the Great Depression, when poverty was apparent everywhere, students on many campuses organized the Association of Hoboes. Members pledged not to spend money unnecessarily and were not allowed to borrow. Dates for members consisted of hikes instead of trips to the movies, and meetings at the school library instead of in town.

## Martian Attack

College students were not always so cynical and skeptical. Literally hundreds of students called home for reassurance that the Martians were not attacking the world on Sunday, October 30, 1938. This was the day the famous H.G. Wells' *War of the Worlds* was dramatized on radio by Orson Welles, and caused many people in the country to believe the "Martian attack" was a real news broadcast.

### Aid for Critics

While student evaluation of professors was grudgingly accepted by many college administrations in the mid-1960s, a committee at Cornell University in 1965 actually suggested that students be given "technical and financial aid" in making up the questionnaires, analyzing the results and preparing the report. No further action beyond this "suggestion" was ever taken.

### Build That School!

Not every college had wealthy benefactors to endow it with stately buildings, dorms and recreation centers. On Campus Day, 1906, classes were suspended at the University of Washington, so that the male faculty and student body could don work clothes and improve campus grounds by digging ditches, clearing the brush, and laying new walks. Being that it was still early in the century, women were relegated to making the hearty meal that followed.

At Tuskegee Institute, founded in 1881 by the great black educator Booker T. Washington as a school to train black teachers (choosing as his site a plantation abandoned after the Civil War), students learned the building trade by helping to erect part of their own institution. In 1903, Tuskegee finally found a benefactor in the person of Andrew Carnegie, who endowed it with $600,000.

### Thesis Time

One of the most impressive theses of all time has to be William F. Buckley's, *God and Man at Yale,* which was later published and became a bestseller.

### Sorority Facts

Alpha Delta Pi is the oldest sorority in America, founded at Wesleyan College in 1851 as the Adelphean Society. Next came Phi Mu, also founded at Wesleyan in 1852, in this case originally named the Philomathean Society. The third oldest sisterhood group was Kappa Alpha Theta, founded in 1870, and considered to be the first recognized Greek Letter *Fraternity* for women.

### First Woman Graduate

The first woman to be granted a diploma by a woman's college was Catherine Brewer Benson, who graduated from Wesleyan College on July 16, 1840.

## The First School for Black Students

In 1867, Union General Oliver O. Howard took an overlooked group of college hopefuls in his hands when he opened Howard University, which was mostly, if not all, black. Before many schools discarded their policy of discrimination in admittance, Howard was a fine university where black men could attend classes without controversy. General Howard, who had lost his right arm in the Civil War battle at Fair Oaks, was a man long devoted to helping black causes, and for a while served as the chief commissioner of President Andrew Johnson's Freedman's Bureau. After Howard, the General went on to found Lincoln Memorial University in Tennessee.

## Yale

In 1701, a collegiate school at Killington (now Clinton), Connecticut was chartered and later moved in 1716 to New Haven, in the same state. In 1718, Cotton Mather wrote to a wealthy English merchant named Elihu Yale and suggested that he could have this school named after him if he was to make a substantial donation. Elihu Yale gave the school a parcel of goods, later sold for the sum of £562—the largest single gift Yale College received until 1837. Yale was started as a stern Puritan school, and was not considered a university until 1887. But its rivalry, good-natured or otherwise, with Harvard, was clear from the beginning. The annual Yale-Harvard boat race (since 1852) and the Yale-Harvard football games (since 1875) are enduring events of college life.

## Whiffenpoofers

Yale University's famous *Whiffenpoof Song* was in actuality adapted from the poem "Gentlemen-Rankers" from Rudyard Kipling's *Barrack Room Ballads.*

## William and Mary

In 1691, James Blair, a missionary sent from the Anglican Church to colonial Virginia, traveled back to England to petition for a college to train clergymen. The school was chartered in 1693 and named after the ruling monarchs, William and Mary. It opened in 1694, and James Blair became its first president. It was subsequently closed three times during the American Revolution, so it could serve as a barracks and strategic post for the army. William and Mary developed many traditions which are today an integral part of college life. In 1776, it founded the honor society *Phi Beta Kappa;* in 1779, when it was re-chartered as a university, because of its several colleges, it developed the elective system

General Oliver Otis Howard, after losing his right arm in the Civil War, founded Howard University in 1867 mostly for black men, who were generally overlooked when it came to college education. He also founded Lincoln Memorial University in Harrogate, Tennessee.

(suggested by Thomas Jefferson); and the honor system was also introduced here. It had a reputation of educating future presidents—Jefferson, Monroe and Tyler all attended, and Washington received his first surveyor's license from William and Mary, where he went on to be elected chancellor.

### First TV and FM Studio

In 1950, Syracuse University became the first educational institution in the world to establish a full-fledged television studio. VVTV, a multi-channel cable TV system, is still in operation today and is run entirely by the students.

Syracuse can also boast the first college FM radio station, WAER, which first hit the airwaves in 1947.

### About Student Newspapers

There are about 1,500 college and university newspapers in the U.S. today. The first campus paper was a weekly news sheet published at Dartmouth College in 1839. The Yale Daily News became the second in 1873.

Student newspapers are certainly big business, printing almost seven million copies across the country each week.

The controversy surrounding the war in Vietnam was hardly the first time campus newspapers got involved in political activity. Back in the 1930s, many newspapers opposed compulsory ROTC programs on campus. In the '30s and '40s, the newspapers came out against college communist organizations. And during the 1950s, many college papers became the first to raise the issue of civil rights.

Henry O. Flipper was the first black to graduate from West Point. In 1877, he led the 10th Cavalry for an 86-hour march through Texas when they almost died from lack of water.

### First Degrees to Blacks

Amherst and Bowdoin Colleges became the first schools to graduate black men in 1826. The first black woman to earn a B.A. was in the Oberlin graduating class of 1862.

### The Real First School

Although Harvard, originally founded in 1636 as Newtowne College (with the sole purpose of preparing men for the ministry), is thought of as the first American college, this is actually not the case. Although Harvard is the oldest *surviving* college, the first school founded in the United States never saw a graduating class. It was established at Henricopolis, Virginia, in 1619, and was forced to cease operation because of the Indian massacres of 1622.

### Music Education

In the 1920s, three important endowments created institutions for professional music training at a higher level than had previously been available in the United States. These gifts helped to open the Eastman School of Music at the University of Rochester, the Juilliard School in New York in 1924, and the Curtis Institute in Philadelphia.

## First State System

The University of the State of New York (SUNY) became the first state university system in 1784. It had no campus, but was rather an organization of various small New York colleges.

## Storing Students

In 1974, William James McGill, president of Columbia University, warned against the danger of using universities "as storage houses for bored young people."

## Naming Brown

Brown University was chartered in 1764 as Rhode Island College. After the Revolutionary War, this school, the smallest of the later-named "Ivy Leaguers," advertised that it would assume the name of any person who could help the institution out by donating $6,000. Nicholas Brown, a Providence merchant, won the title with his bid of $5,000.

## Yale and Vassar

Did you know that in 1966, Yale tried to convince Vassar to move from Poughkeepsie over to New Haven, thus joining the two schools? Vassar finally said a firm, "No."

Nicholas Brown paid only $5,000 to get his name on a university which had been called Rhode Island College. He answered an ad asking for donations in 1840.

■ Great Events ■

At a time when some whites felt that "the only good Indian is a dead Indian," Hampton Institute in Virginia, a black college, accepted Indians.

## Princeton in the Beginning

Princeton was founded as the College of New Jersey in 1746. Its first president, John Witherspoon, was the only clergyman to sign the Declaration of Independence. During Witherspoon's reign as president, Princeton produced 39 Representatives in the House, 21 Senators, 12 Governors, a Vice-President, and a President (Madison). From June 26 to November 4, 1783, Nassau Hall, the main building of the college, served as the nation's capital and as housing for colonial troops.

A few days after the Boston Tea Party (1774), Princeton students made a replica bonfire of the tea supply at the college. In 1807, 125 of the total 200 students were expelled for rioting. The Princeton rebellion of 1817 saw students lock their tutors in their rooms, while they went around setting fire to all the outhouses.

## Patriotic Penn

The University of Pennsylvania, another Ivy-League College, was founded in 1749 by Benjamin Franklin. In 1765, the college began the first medical school in North America, thus becoming the first university on the continent. Twenty members of the Continental Congress were Penn alumni, faculty or trustees. Nine Penn-affiliated patriots signed the Declaration of Independence.

## About Dartmouth

Dartmouth, the only *college* left in the Ivy League group, founded in 1769 as a school for "Indians and Children of Pagans," had a first graduating class of four students, which included the son of the founder of the school, Eleazar Wheelock. The legend that any Indian with the proper record upon applying for admission to Dartmouth will be admitted tuition-free is just that—a legend.

## Porky Athletes

In 1980, researchers at the University of California at San Diego monitored the heartbeats of pigs running on a treadmill as an experiment in body endurance. One ambitious pig ran the mile in less than eight minutes!

## Familiar Quotes

John Bartlett's book of Familiar Quotations began when the young man of 16 found a job, in 1836, at Harvard's University bookstore. In the 13 years it took him to save enough money to buy the bookstore, he read almost every book in it. In 1855, using printers from the university, he himself published 1,000 copies of his book of quotes, a now-famous literary institution.

## The Seven Sisters

The female counterpart of the Ivy League, the group of colleges referred to as the Seven Sisters comprises Barnard, Bryn Mawr, Mount Holyoke, Radcliffe, Smith, Vassar and Wellesley. The group was established first as the Four College Conference in 1911. When Barnard, Bryn Mawr and Radcliffe later joined, it became the Seven Colleges Conference. This group met to discuss methods and ideas for the future of female education in America.

## Think Tank

The government of France, in appreciation of the Vassar alumnae's efforts during World War I, shipped the college a 42,000-pound, 16-man tank. It stayed on the Vassar fields until 1934. History does not record just how it was moved off or where.

"The Day the Ice Goes Out of the River" is celebrated by the consuming of ice cream cones at St. Cloud State University in central Minnesota. Whatever the weather, the students dress for Spring.

# VI. Sex

### The Frailer Sex

Dr. Edward Hammond Clarke, a physician and Harvard graduate, wrote a book in 1873 called *Sex in Education*. Its publication caused much furor and debate at the time and set the tone for women's education in that era. In the book, the good doctor protested that a woman's health could be ruined by attending college, being that the female of the species was frailer by nature and had specific health problems. Although parents still permitted their daughters to attend college, women's schools were known to become highly protective and almost motherly in their pampering procedures.

### Sexual Attitudes Today

In 1965, women on college campuses who felt that sex with a number of men was a sinful activity to pursue comprised 70% of their population. By 1975, the proportion had dropped to 37%.

Men felt that sex with many partners was wrong in proportions of 58% in 1965. By 1975, that figure was down to 20%.

### Kinsey Reports

Alfred Kinsey, a noted biologist, began his famous sexual research program at his Institute for Sex Research, on the Indiana University campus. His books, *Sexual Behavior in the Human Male* (1948) and *Sexual Behavior in the Human Female* (1953) have become the foundations of all the studies that followed. At the time of Kinsey's studies, 27% of the young women and 67% of the young men interviewed had already had at least one sexual experience.

### Chaperoning Dates

The 1930s ushered in a new liberalism on campus. At Dartmouth, students went on their dates unchaperoned—for the first time—until 11 P.M. Yale undergraduates had only to obtain written permission from their deans or the campus police in order to entertain female visitors

**Smith College has always been exclusively for women, right up through the revolution of the 60s, but it did not appoint a woman president—Jill Ker Conway—until 1975.**

until 6 P.M. At Harvard, the "two-women" rule specified that Harvard men had to invite along a second girl on dates.

### Should Men and Women Share Everything?

When women were admitted to colleges and universities which were formerly all-male, few colleges had separate bathrooms and toilets for women.

Many put in separate sanitary facilities, but in some colleges, such as the University of Massachusetts, men and women were prohibited from sharing dormitory bathrooms. In 1981, seventy students of U Mass protested by staying in an administration building as a demonstration which might be called a strike. The effort was unsuccessful and the seventy students were allowed to leave their posts without being disciplined for violations.

In other places the battle is still going on for sharing bathrooms in dormitories.

### Watching Out for Women

Until 1917 there existed a position at Vassar called the Lady Principal, whose job it was to interview the girls' male callers, advise on matters of dress and bathing habits, and generally supervise the girls' conduct. Vassar did not eliminate the 10 P.M. bedtime rule until 1910, and did not let ladies attend the movies unchaperoned until 1917.

## Harvard Law and Ladies

The first woman president of the *Harvard Law Review* was elected in 1976.

## First Female President at Smith

Although Smith was a girls' school and chose throughout the 60's to remain so, even when other women's schools were starting to admit men, the first woman president of Smith, Jill Ker Conway, was not appointed until 1975!

## Pregnant Students

The greatest number of college student pregnancies occurred in the mid-1940s, as thousands of World War II veterans sought to complete their interrupted college careers and brought their wives along on campus with them. By 1946, Cornell reported that it had more than 500 children on campus. The University of Illinois expected many more than the 800 they already had at that time.

## The Girl Next Door

According to a survey conducted by the *Amherst Student* news bulletin, of the 1,427 married Amherst men attending classes from the years of 1900 to 1972, some 838 had Smith wives and 589 had Mount Holyoke wives. That meant that 58.7% of the men married girls from Smith, and the remaining 41.2% married women from Mount Holyoke. Only 0.1% married females from other colleges or from no college at all. Since all three schools occupy the same area in central Massachusetts, these figures would seem to imply that Amherst men prefer staying close to home when selecting future mates.

## Pulitzer Ladies

Vassar boasts an impressive record of four Pulitzer Prize winners among their alumni—Edna St. Vincent Millay in 1923; Elizabeth Bishop in 1956; Lucinda Franks in 1971; and Margaret Leech in 1942 and 1960. Vassar holds the record, therefore, for the most Pulitzer Prizes among women graduates—five.

## Co-Ed at Yale

In 1969 in the fall, 580 women entered Yale, making the school coeducational for the first time. The first woman to head a department at the school was Anne Coffin Hanson, in art history, whose appointment went through in 1974. For the class of 1973, some 2,847 women applied to Yale—admission was granted to 288 or 10%.

### Stop Those Cuddles!

The dean of the University of North Dakota in 1920 put a ban on "cheek-to-cheek dancing, unnecessary clinging, cuddling, or dancing the shimmy." At one point, there was even a student committee called the Women's Senate of Secret Observers, who reported on incidents involving the above offenses.

### Baring the Knees

For some reason lost through the ravages of time, bare-knee kissing enjoyed wide popularity on the Brown University campus during the 1920s.

### Blind Dates

In 1920, Wellesley students organized a "blind-date syndicate" which saw to it that no one would go dateless if they didn't want to. The organization charged 50¢ a date, 25¢ additional if the date called back afterwards, and $1 if the date included dinner. All proceeds were donated to the college's semi-centennial celebration.

### The Science of Co-Ed

One of the first major schools in the country to reject the idea of female intellectual inferiority and to accept both men and women as full-time students in a totally co-educational atmosphere, was the Massachusetts Institute of Technology. The school opened in 1861 and was completely co-ed by 1890.

### Cheap Thrills

Ohio's Oberlin College now offers its students a 60% discount on over-the-counter birth-control items, thanks to a recently-formed contraceptive cooperative. At the co-op, a dozen condoms, normally priced at $4.80 plus tax, sell for a mere $1.70.

### Polly Arrives

Carroll College in Wisconsin (Fred MacMurray's alma mater), took a decisive move toward co-education and the elimination of sexism when they decided to make certain alterations in the personality of the school's mascot. Until 1970, it had been Petey Pioneer. In that year they gave him a friend—Polly Pioneer.

Ezra Cornell, in the campus Quad, has never moved an inch, since his statue was placed there. Does this have significance? See below.

## First Co-Ed Dorm

The first co-ed dormitory in the country was located at the University of Oregon in Eugene. It was called Friendly Hall, and it went co-ed in 1893. Still standing as a campus building, it is no longer used as a dorm.

## Passing Virgins

Practically every school in the country has a "passing virgin" legend, but Cornell's goes like this: Rumor has it that the statue of Ezra Cornell and the statue of Andrew Dickinson White in the campus Quad will leave their pedestals and shake hands whenever a young lady uninitiated in the ways of love passes by. The legend goes on to say that they have not been able to shake hands even once.

### Forced to Female

Matthew Vassar, the brewer who endowed Vassar College, had originally intended to give his money to a local hospital before he was finally persuaded to found a college for young women.

The spinster, Sophia Smith, whose brother swore that not a penny of his money would go toward women's education, was persuaded by her pastor, John M. Greene, to endow Smith College, one of the few women's colleges to remain all female to this day.

### Co-Ed Gains

Going co-ed seems to provide nothing but benefits to previously single-sex colleges. At Westminster College in Fulton, Missouri, three years of co-education has produced a 100-point rise in applicants' average College Board scores. By admitting women, Kenyon College in Gambier, Ohio, tripled its enrollment—from 500 in the early 60s to 1,450 today—without losing its reputation as a highly selective school.

### Women What?

To avoid calling early female students freshmen, Elmira College called them *protomathians* and Rutgers Female College (later Douglass College) used the term "novian." Vassar settled on calling their first-year students, "first-year students."

### Where the Boys Are

The subject areas in college containing the greatest proportion of male students are dentistry, where 86% are male; and engineering, where 89.4% are male.

### Double Date

Bob Khayat, a football star at the University of Mississippi in the late 1950s, may have set some kind of undergraduate record when he managed to get dates with both Lynda Lee Mead and Mary Ann Mobley. These Ole Miss co-eds both became Miss America titlists.

### Military Co-Eds

Although Vassar College did not start admitting men on a regular basis until 1969, 40 war veterans (all men) were admitted in April 1946 on a special basis as full-time students.

### Co-Ed Is Current

According to a 1972 survey of the 298 women's colleges which had been in existence as such in 1960, only 49% have remained exclusively female.

Vassar went co-ed in 1969; in 1975, Harvard and Radcliffe combined their degrees and programs; Sarah Lawrence and Bennington accepted males in 1968; and Skidmore followed suit in 1971.

## Campus Sins

"Sex irregularity" was voted the worst sin on campus by the students of the University of Texas during the years 1919 to 1921. The runners-up were stealing, cheating, lying, drinking, and gambling.

## Dance Fever

Social dancing was outlawed on most college campuses until the 1920s. At the rare, highly-chaperoned dances, students had to obey the infamous "Two-Foot Rule," which specified that the distance between dancing couples be at least two feet. Apparently, some young ladies saw fit to carry rulers with them.

There were some earlier instances of co-ed dancing. Smith girls, for one, were allowed their first "mixed dancing promenade" as early as 1894. Vassar followed in 1897, but Mount Holyoke held out until 1913, relenting only when the student body threatened to wear black all the time if they were not allowed to have males at their dances.

# VII. College Life Today

### Killer, Anyone?

The main game played around U.S. campuses today is no longer goldfish-swallowing, telephone-booth-stuffing or co-ed softball—it's something considerably more lethal. It's called "Killer," and it involves students in an ambitious manhunt to "kill" the other players with rubber-tipped dart guns before they can themselves be eliminated from the game (assassinated). The student who is left standing wins, and enjoys a certain amount of prestige for doing so. All sorts of traps and ruses are set for the players in order to lead them to their "demise."

The game began in 1965 at the University of Michigan after the release of a film by Carlo Ponti called "The Tenth Victim," which was set in a futuristic society where people kill for sport and competition. The idea was brought to the school by Lenny Pitt, a student and residential director who felt that the game would be useful in getting freshmen better acquainted with one another. The game has since infiltrated scores of campuses, including all the Ivy League ones.

At the University of Pennsylvania, where nonviolence seems to still be the keynote, the game has been modified. Here, it is called "Kisser," and this version culminates in the victims having chocolate candy kisses thrown at them.

### The College Game (on Board)

At Stanford University in Palo Alto, California, they're playing the Stanford Game, a board game somewhat on the order of Monopoly but not concerned with accumulating money. The idea is to get through college.

On the way around the board, you collect points or lose points depending on whether you pass or fail certain courses (such as human sexuality), get good grades, read the campus daily paper (the game contains a mini-version of one issue), or have to go back and pass a special

What college has the most bikes? Might be University of California at Santa Barbara, which encourages bike riding to class. They have counted 12,000. The campus has five miles of bikeways with underpasses.

major course. Some squares you might land on would give you a year overseas to study, have a good time off campus, or live the lifecycle of a "nerd." You roll dice to see where you are going to land.

The game, invented by two alumni, might have most appeal to other alumni, and perhaps they can more easily afford the high ($20) price tag.

### Arts at Indiana

Besides being renowned for having one of the finest music departments in the country, and for having been the location used for the recent film, *Breaking Away,* Indiana University at Bloomington is a haven for opera buffs. A different opera is produced each week on the campus and even continues during the summer . . . making Indiana U. possibly the only place in the world where one can see an opera presented every week of the year.

### Cheap Schools

Did you know that there are more than 1,200 U.S. colleges where tuition is less than $750 a year for state residents? Many of these schools charge less than $300. Some can cost less than $100 a year and more than 50 charge nothing at all. You can get the names and addresses of these schools in a booklet titled, *Under $750: A Student's Guide to 1,215 Low-Tuition Colleges,* available from your local library.

### Suicide Rate

It is a fact that only 10% of all colleges have their own mental health services. Yet students, who sometimes become severely depressed over marks or loneliness at college, are 50% more likely to kill themselves than people their age in general. In California, where the college enrollment has been the fastest and the proportion of young people who go to college the highest, the suicide rate of youths 15 to 24 doubled between 1960 and 1970.

According to the best estimates, about 1,000 college students do away with themselves every year—and about 10,000 attempt suicide. Over 100,000 threaten to do it.

### World News

According to a study released in 1981 by the Educational Testing Service, college students have little knowledge of international affairs. Most of the 3,000 students surveyed in the study, conducted at 185 institutions, received what would have been failing grades on a world

At Gallaudet College in Washington, D.C., deaf students are taught lip-reading and given auditory training with electronic equipment.

events test given by the educational service. Of the 101 questions asked, less than 15% of the students got two-thirds right!

### Educational "Flash"

The library at Indiana University in Bloomington has recently been the target of "flashers," who expose more than knowledge to startled students. Library officials have been forced to install a police force, which they say is on the lookout for "vandalism, consumption of food and drink and uncommon sex . . ."

### Enroll!

To encourage enrollment, colleges have begun to take some drastic steps. At Kent State University, radio commercial time was bought. In 1973 at Northern Kentucky State College, during Christmas vacation, representatives launched 200 helium balloons—103 of which carried scholarship offers on the basis of finders keepers.

### Job Problem

The situation became tighter and tighter in the 1970s for college graduates trying to find jobs. For example, according to 1975 Department of Labor statistics, there were an estimated 4,300 new job openings for

Ohio State students—4,378 of them—set the Guinness record for the largest musical chairs game in Columbus on April 27, 1980.

psychologists. In that same year, colleges turned out 58,430 students with a B.A. in psychology, 10% of which would be going on for their master's degrees.

### Brown's Papers

Brown University is the smallest school in the country with a daily paper. Its *Fresh Fruit Magazine,* another school publication, published on a weekly basis, boasts a circulation of 50,000 readers throughout Rhode Island. And the university's chorus was the first college performing group in the U.S. to be invited into the People's Republic of China.

### Popular Class

The nation's first (and only) department of Popular Culture was established in 1980 at Bowling Green University in Kentucky. Ray B. Browne, founder of a group called the Popular Culture Association and chairman of the department, believes there is a lot to be learned from Burger King, *Valley of the Dolls,* and Archie Bunker. His class reads romance novels and torrid bestsellers; they perform and study soap operas in class; and take occasional field trips down to fast-food restaurants, where they take notes on the rituals people go through while ordering a hamburger. Most people they question, however, insist that they are unaware of any great sociological import to their action. "I was just coming in to get a hamburger," they inevitably claim. Last spring, Browne himself published a monograph on the sociological importance of the toilet in the work of a minor 1920s writer.

### Natural Habitat

Anthropology and social science majors at the University of California at Irvine recently invited a Colombian family to live on a small plot of land off from the rest of the campus (called "The Farm") in order to observe them living in the natural habitat they constructed there.

### Money, Anyone?

According to Ed Rosenwasser, owner of Student College Aid, a computer service that matches up students with available scholarship funds, over $100 million of student aid currently goes unused. His data bank contains information on $500 million in nongovernment aid and over $2 billion in government grants and scholarships.

Trying for a Guinness World Record in the category of bed pushing, students at Saint Vincent College in Latrobe, Pennsylvania, used a hospital bed with an extra bicycle size wheel, as the rules allow.

## About Attendance

Sixty percent of today's high school graduates pursue some form of higher education, though only 50% of these students stay long enough to collect a degree.

The proportion of college graduates between the ages of 25 and 29 has grown to nearly 24%. In other words, one out of every four young adults will have obtained a college degree.

And according to a 10-year-old Gallup Poll, only 15% of parents questioned wanted their children to attend college in order to receive mental stimulation—an overwhelming 44% desired college for their offspring so that they could get better jobs in the future.

## The Intellectual Elite

According to Charles Kadushin in his recent study of the 172 men and women with the most intellectual clout in the United States (called *The American Intellectual Elite*), 50% of them are connected in some way with either Columbia, Harvard, Yale or New York University.

## Money Troubles

Stanford University recently announced that the cost of tuition, fees, room and board for a single year will rise 13.3% over the previous year, from $8,921 to $10,105. At Harvard, one dean forecasts an increase of 11% to 15% above the present $9,170. Matters are bound to get even pricier. A new study on Williams College projects that by 1990, tuition, room and board will total $16,890 a year!

## The Largest Gift

If you're looking for financial assistance, you may be well advised to try Buena Vista College in Storm Lake, Iowa. The school received an anonymous contribution of $18 million in May, 1980. Rounding it out, it comes to about $14,000 per student, and that makes it the highest per-capita gift ever made to a college. The tuition for the school runs about $3,225 per year.

## Vetoing the Haze

In December, 1980, New Jersey governor Brendan Byrne signed legislation setting stiff penalties for college students who participate in the traditional fraternity initiation rite known as "hazing." Attending the signing was Dorothy Flowers, whose son William was buried alive and died on November 12, 1974, at Monmouth College in a 6-foot-deep sandpit as part of a college fraternity initiation. The penalty for breaking the law was set at a 6-month jail term or a $1,000 fine.

Spalding College in Louisville, Kentucky, commemorated its 60th anniversary with a huge birthday card to itself on October 3, 1980. It covered 8,839½ square feet.

■ College Life Today ■ 91

The world record in 1979 for the largest ice cream sundae was set by the students of the Mark Twain Summer Institute in Clayton, Missouri. Total weight of 1,616 lbs. did not include 90 lbs. of nuts, 250 lbs. of chocolate, 250 lbs. of strawberry topping and 65.6 lbs. of instant whip. Their record was surpassed in 1981 by high school students in Troy, Ohio, with a 10,808-lb. mountain of ice cream.

## The Facts and Figures

Today, the total enrollment in colleges and universities across the country is 11,260,092. This figure is made up of 5,640,998 men and 5,619,094 women. There are 8,785,893 students in private universities, and 2,474,199 in public institutions. In 1978–9, there were 3,134 colleges, universities and branch campuses to house these students. Sixty-three percent attend full-time.

The demographic breakdown is as follows:
52.5% men
10.5% black
53.0% have parents who make over $15,000 per year
80.0% have parents who have both graduated from high school
42.0% have a father who graduated from college
20.0% have a mother who graduated from college
10.0% are atheists.

## More Facts and Figures

52% of all students who drop out of college do so because of lack of money

71% of all students who dropped out did not care whether they graduated or not

68% of college students drink beer

51% of all male students have at least one beer every day

20% of all female students have at least one beer every day

Only 6.5% of all students had an A or A+ average in high school—the biggest chunk, 27.5%, had a B− average in high school.

## Ethnic Education

The Jewish people in the United States have the largest proportion of their ethnic group attending college. According to a Gallup Poll, 58% of all Jews have graduated from college.

**The highest prime number, in case anyone wants to know, consists of 13,395 digits, as Harry Nelson, 47, and David Slowinski, 25, found out at the University of California's Livermore Laboratory's Cray One Computer.**

•

The world's longest slide rule, longer than a football field (323 feet long), is laid out in the University of Illinois College of Law Building in Champaign. Built by Greg Maggs and Robert Kolstad, it was completed on November 11, 1979.

94 ■ College Records ■

At the Duke University Medical Center in Durham, North Carolina, students have been simulating underwater dives in an 8-foot spherical chamber, using a gas mixture that contained nitrogen, oxygen and helium. In 1980, three men reached a "depth" of 2,132 feet, and on February 3, 1981, three men (including one from the first group) reached 2,250 feet in a 43-day trial.

### The Future of College Grads

Whereas a college education once was an assurance of a high income after graduation, this is no longer the case. According to the U.S. Bureau of the Census, humanities graduates are the hardest hit, getting starting salaries of $10–12,000 per year—a figure which has increased the least of any field over the last ten years.

College grads, on the whole, are still marginally better off than nongrads. The median yearly income, as reported in 1979, demonstrates this fact:

College Graduates, 24 and younger = $9,000 per year
High School Graduates, 24 and younger = $7,000 per year
College Graduates, 45 and older = $17,600 per year
High School Graduates, 45 and older = $10,900 per year

College teachers seem to have a higher overall average. Their median income is currently at around $22,000 per year.

## Things You Never Would Have Guessed About College Students Today

According to a 1980 U.C.L.A.-sponsored "American Freshman" survey:

☐ One out of every four sophomores claim to be a born-again Christian. The same number jog for exercise.

☐ More students think gay rights should be outlawed than believe pot should be legalized.

☐ For every one woman who wanted to go into law, medicine, engineering or business 10 years ago, there are five women today.

☐ Students in 1980 were less interested in "developing a philosophy of life" than they were in gaining "money, status, and power."

☐ 2.2% of all students don't ever want to be employed.

☐ 2% plan to drop out of school.

☐ The majority of students are against pollution and for the death penalty.

☐ About half of all college attendees think sex is "okay, if the people really like each other."

☐ College students are the most surveyed group in the country.

☐ They watch two hours and seven minutes of TV each day.

☐ They vastly prefer Pepsi to Perrier water.

# VIII. College Sports

## FOOTBALL

### First Century Report

According to N.C.A.A. figures, when college football celebrated its first century—1869-1969—an estimated 900 teams had used about two and a half million players in 325,000 games. There were approximately 750 million fans at those games.

### First and Last Games of the Century

Rutgers defeated Princeton, 6 goals to 4, in football's first game on Nov. 6, 1869. There were 25 players on a side at the time. Though football later became known for having 11 men on a side, college football's first century ended with the last bowl game, the Orange Bowl on Jan. 1, 1969, with 12 men on one side. That's how many men Kansas had on the field when Penn State was going for its conversion at the end of the contest. Penn State got a second chance because of the penalty, made 2 points, and beat Kansas, 15-14.

### The Ivy League

Much legend and awe surrounds the name "Ivy League," as it refers to the eight schools included within it. The term is often associated with family money, prestige and high academic standing. In actuality, the league was not officially started until 1954 as the "Ivy Group," between the eight participating colleges most influential in college football. It served as a means of standardizing and regulating collegiate football games.

### Ban Football!

Although remembered as one of the most athletic of presidents, Theodore Roosevelt threatened to ban college football in 1905. Eighteen players had died of injuries that year and 73 were seriously hurt. One of Roosevelt's sons, a freshman at Harvard, came home from the

Amos Alonzo Stagg was rightly called "The Grand Old Man of Football," as he spent 74 of his 102 years playing or coaching. Stagg was the first to use a shift, huddle, quick kick and center snap with his teams.

first day of practice with a black eye. At the President's urging, the flying wedge was outlawed as a move, and a neutral zone between opposing lines was instituted. Roosevelt's demands to outlaw rough play led to the Rules Committee legalizing the forward pass in 1906.

## Team Nicknames

The most popular nicknames for college football teams among the 140 or so major-college division schools are "Tigers" and "Bulldogs," with seven each. The "Tigers" are: Auburn, Clemson, Louisiana State, Memphis State, Missouri, University of the Pacific and Princeton. The "Bulldogs" are: The Citadel, Drake, Fresno State, Georgia, Louisiana Tech, Mississippi State and Yale.

Another candidate for the most popular name would have been "Indians," except for some technical difficulties. One difficulty is that two schools, sensitive to the American Indians' rights and image of themselves, changed their nicknames in the past few years—Dartmouth from "Indians" to "Big Green" and Stanford from "Indians" to "Cardinals." The only major-college football teams that retain "Indians" are Arkansas State and William & Mary. Many others prefer more specific Indian names, such as the Central Michigan "Chippewas," San Diego State "Aztecs," Eastern Michigan "Hurons," Miami University "Redmen," Florida State "Seminoles," Utah "Utes," and so on.

Among *all* colleges playing football, the nickname popularity closely follows the major-college thinking. In order, the most used nicknames are: "Tigers" (27), "Bulldogs" and "Bears" (17 each), "Wildcats" (16) and "Eagles" (13).

Most educational nickname (or the best way to stay in good graces with the faculty): Glassboro State "Profs."

## Oldest Coach Ever

Amos Alonzo Stagg coached until 1960, when he was 98 years old. His teams, which were at Springfield College (then the International Y.M.C.A. School), the University of Chicago, and the College of the Pacific (now University of the Pacific) from 1890–1946, won 314 games. After the Pacific job, he was an assistant to his son, Amos Jr., at Susquehanna University, for five years, then was a special kicking coach at Stockton Junior College, in California, until 1960. He died in 1965 at age 102.

## Best Head Coaching Debut

In 1948, Bennie Oosterbaan, an assistant coach at Michigan, his alma mater, was elevated to head coach. He won all nine games and the national championship, becoming the first and only man to do that as a first-year head coach.

When Bennie Oosterbaan played for Michigan in the 1920s, he starred as a pass-catching end and had no idea he would go down in football history as a coach.

Jim Thorpe, an American Indian, played football at Carlisle (1907-08 and 1911-12) excelling in many phases of the game. He was unanimously selected to the All-Time Team and consensus All-America in 1911-12.

### Only Player to Have Town Named After Him

In 1954, the small Pennsylvania communities of Lower Mauch Chunk, Upper Mauch Chunk and East Mauch Chunk consolidated and named their community after Jim Thorpe, the alltime All-American from the former Indian training school in Carlisle, Pennsylvania, that competed on the college level in sports. The name of the 5,300-population town: Jim Thorpe, Pennsylvania.

### "The Rock" Gets a Rock in His Honor

The small village of Voss, Norway, honored Knute Rockne, the Norwegian who became famous as the Notre Dame football coach, with a downtown memorial. The memorial includes a huge rock (Rockne's nickname was "Rock") surrounded by eleven stones.

### Producing Coaches

No school can match Miami University, in Ohio, for turning out great coaches. Considering men who played and/or coached there, the list of former Miamians sounds like a page out of the Football Hall of

The man who made Notre Dame (and himself) famous in the annals of football was Coach Knute Rockne, whose teams defeated the best in the nation year after year in the 1920s. He was killed in a plane crash in 1931.

Fame. For starters, the former Miamians who have been named national "Coach of the Year," either by the American Football Coaches Association or the Football Writers Association of America are (with the teams they coached when they won the award):

1946 Earl Blaik, Army
1957 Woody Hayes, Ohio State
1958 Paul Dietzel, Louisiana State
1964 Ara Parseghian, Notre Dame
1967 John Pont, Indiana
1968 Woody Hayes, Ohio State
1969 Bo Schembechler, Michigan
1975 Woody Hayes, Ohio State

Among the other Miamians were Paul Brown and Weeb Ewbank, both of whom won championships with professional teams; Sid Gillman, a successful pro coach with three different teams; Stu Holcomb, formerly of Purdue; George Blackburn, who coached Virginia; Bill Arnsparger, New York Giants; Carmen Cozza, Yale; Bill Mallory, Colorado; Jim Root, William & Mary, and Dick Crum, North Carolina.

### Oldest Current Coach

Ralph McKinzie, at 87 in 1981, was listed as assistant coach for Eureka College, Illinois, the school where he began as a player in 1916, and became a coach after he was graduated. McKinzie, who also coached at Northern Illinois during his long career, was the head coach at Eureka a half-century ago, and the field was named after him as early as 1933. His most famous player: Ronald Reagan, who graduated in 1932.

### First Big-Time Football Teams to Select Black Head Coach

When Wichita State, in 1979, named Willie Jeffries as the head football coach, he became the first black to coach at a major-college level. In 1981, Dennis Green became Northwestern's head coach, and thus the second black at a big-time level.

### First White Head Coach at a Predominantly Black College

Joe Purzycki was named head coach at Delaware State for the 1981 season, becoming what is believed to be the first white to coach at a predominantly black school.

### All-Around Coach

When John Heisman was of college age, he was one of the first football players to earn letters from two different schools—Brown in 1887–89 and Penn in 1890–91. That set him off on his coaching travels in which he is believed to have been a head coach at more schools than any man. Heisman coached at eight, including Oberlin twice. He began at Oberlin in 1892, went to Akron (then called Buchtel) in 1893, and back to Oberlin in 1894. From there, Heisman headed south for stints at Auburn, 1895–99; Clemson, 1900–03; Georgia Tech, 1904–19; and east to Penn, 1920–22; and Washington & Jefferson, 1923. He finished his coaching career at Rice in Texas, 1924–27. His overall record was an impressive 184 victories, 68 defeats and 16 ties.

But he is better known for lending his name to the most famous individual award in American sports—the Heisman Trophy. Incidently, it wasn't until 1971, when Pat Sullivan of Auburn got the award, that the Heisman Trophy, first given in 1935, went to a player from one of the many schools where Heisman coached.

### Going Professional

Though there are no official records for the colleges that produce the most professional players, it is believed that the 1980 University of Pittsburgh team had the most players signed to National Football League contracts. Twelve Pitt players were drafted by the pros and another seven signed as free agents.

The 1970 Ohio State team had 13 players drafted.

The 1947 Notre Dame team is said to have had 53 players on campus,

From All-America football at the University of Colorado to the Supreme Court of the U.S. is the course Byron "Whizzer" White (left) took. With him is Billy "White Shoes" Johnson of Widener College (Chester, Pennsylvania) who set Division III rushing records by averaging 10.5 yards per carry in the 1972 season and 9.09 yards per rush for his career (1971-73).

including freshmen who were not yet eligible and underclassmen who were not playing much, go on to pro football.

The 1966 Michigan State team had the distinction of having three of its senior stars—defensive lineman Bubba Smith, linebacker George Webster and receiver Gene Washington—being selected the very first three men in the draft.

Terry Bradshaw, of Louisiana Tech, in 1970, and Buck Buchanan, of Grambling, in 1963, were the only small-college players to become the very first player taken in the annual pro draft. Both became superstars and leaders of Super Bowl championship teams.

The first player taken in the first pro draft, in 1936, was Jay Ber-

**"Old 98," Michigan's Tom Harmon, went through 47 jerseys during his college career to set an unofficial, but probable, record, and this picture shows why.**

wanger of the University of Chicago. He never played professional football.

The school with the most of its former players now in the National Football League, as of the opening of the 1981 season, was Southern Cal, with 43. Tied for second, with 26 each, were Ohio State, Oklahoma, Penn State and U.C.L.A.

### Jerseys and Jersey Numbers

No official record is available, but it is believed that Tom Harmon, Michigan's Heisman Trophy winning tailback, went through 47 jerseys during his three-year career, 1938–40. His uniform number, 98, was fa-

Number 44 was carried proudly at Syracuse by Jim Brown (left, above), the All-America running back in 1956. That number was later worn by Floyd Little (right, above) at Syracuse, who went on to professional glory also.

mous enough in that era, but Old 98, as he was called, wore what was then called "breakaway jerseys," which would tear easily and enable him to escape would-be tacklers.

The most famous number for a running back may have been the No. 44 worn by Jim Brown when he was an All-America at Syracuse in 1956. That number was also passed on to Ernie Davis, who won the Heisman Trophy for the Orangemen in 1961, and Floyd Little, among other great running backs at the school. Interestingly enough, Brown's number in professional football, 32, later became the most popular number for college running backs, as it is to this day. The most notable was O.J. Simpson, at the University of Southern California.

For a brief surge of popularity, no number was ever as popular as Doak Walker's 37 at Southern Methodist University. The three-time All-America (1947–49) and 1948 Heisman winner was held in such esteem in his home state of Texas that almost every youngster wanted to wear the number. One junior team solved that problem by renaming its team "the 37's."

Best number kept in the same family: 11. That was worn by the three Wistert brothers from Michigan who became All-America tackles—Francis in 1933, Albert in 1942 and Alvin in 1948–49.

■ Football ■ 105

Number 32 at Southern Cal became identified with O. J. Simpson, who was probably the most acclaimed running back of modern times in college.

## Football Jerseys

Cut-off football jerseys began to gain popularity in the early 1900s at the University of Tennessee, because they served to keep the players cool and gave their opponents less to grab on to.

## Equipment

Lafayette University claims that one of its players, George Barclay, invented the football helmet in 1896 to curtail the develoment of cauliflower ears. He pieced together three thick leather straps and wore them in a game against the University of Pennsylvania that season.

### Unusual Jersey Numbers

Yale and Harvard usually take their end-of-the-year clash very seriously, but in 1952 Yale knew it was a far better team. They call it simply "The Game." As it rolled up the score and got another touchdown, Yale substituted No. 99 on the extra-point try. But Yale did not kick the point, choosing instead to send this 140-pounder into the end zone. A pass was thrown to him, and he caught it for the point. Only later did embarrassed Harvard learn that No. 99, Charley Yeager, was Yale's student manager.

### Most Broken Helmets

There is no official records for most broken helmets, but a 1980 Baylor University player, Mike Singletary, went through more than a dozen helmets, including nine in his junior season. Most of the broken helmets by the All-American linebacker were the result of his collisions. He once went through three helmets in three days of practice. According to the team's trainer, however, the broken helmets were a good sign: better the helmet give than the player suffer a concussion.

"Better the helmet than the head!" should be Mike Singletary's motto. The hard-hitting All-America linebacker (#63) from Baylor broke more than a dozen helmets in his college career, including 9 in his junior season.

Coach at Oklahoma during their 1953-57 winning streak was Bud Wilkinson, who later was appointed by the President to head a national sports development program.

## Longest Unbeaten Streaks

The University of Washington compiled 63 consecutive games in which it was not beaten during 1907–17. Including in the streak were four ties. California stopped the streak, 27-0.

The University of Oklahoma won 47 consecutive games from 1953–57 before losing to Notre Dame, 7-0.

## Tieless Streaks

Widener College, a school in Chester, Pennsylvania, had gone 297 games without being tied as of the start of the 1982 season.

## Combination Streaks

For success in *both* football and basketball, nobody can top Wittenberg University, of Springfield, Ohio. Though it does not give scholarships, the Lutheran school with just 2,200 students had 26 straight years of winning football teams and 24 straight seasons of winning basketball teams going into the 1981–82 school year.

## College Football Poll

Since the Associated Press began its poll of sportswriters and sportscasters to rank college teams each week in 1936, a total of 151 different teams have made the top 20 listings, going into the 1981 season. Most frequently listed: Notre Dame. In 44 of 46 years, the Irish have appeared at least once, and they appeared in 398 weekly listings of the total 492 weekly polls. Second in total appearances: Ohio State, with 347. Among some smaller schools who made it at least one week are: Muhlenberg (in 1946), Catawba (1947), Lafayette (three times in 1940), Williams (1942), Washington and Lee (1950) and Bucknell (1951).

## Staying Power in the Football Polls

Four teams—Notre Dame (1943), Army (1945), Nebraska (1971) and Southern Cal (1972)—qualify as having been ranked No. 1 from start to finish of that season. Most times ranked No. 1 in weekly rankings was Notre Dame, with 62, followed by Ohio State, with 45.

## Extinct Bowl Games

At one point, in the late 1940s, there were as many as 47 post-season bowl games. Now there are 16 for major-college teams. Among the most active post-season bowlers was Hardin-Simmons, of Texas, which appeared in the Alamo Bowl (January, 1947); Camellia Bowl (December, 1948); Grape Bowl (December, 1948); Harbor Bowl (January, 1948); and Shrine Bowl (December, 1948).

Among other bowl games no longer in existence were the Bacardi

Before achieving professional fame with the Chicago Bears and quarterbacking them into a 24-game unbeaten streak, Sid Luckman was the most highly regarded player in Columbia football.

Bowl, in Havana, Cuba (Villanova versus Auburn), 1937; the Gotham Bowl, played twice in New York City in the 1960s; Aviation Bowl, in Dayton, Ohio, 1961; Oil Bowl, in Houston, 1946; Raisin Bowl, in Fresno, California, 1946–49; and the Salad Bowl, in Phoenix, Arizona, 1948–52.

### Winningest Bowl Teams

Going into the 1981 football season, Southern California, with 19 victories, was the school with the most bowl victories, followed closely by Alabama, with 18. West Texas State (4–0), Purdue (4–0) and Toledo (3–0) had the best percentages.

### Best Bowl Streak

Alabama, which went to its first bowl in 1926, has been to more bowl games (35) than any team. (Texas is second with 28). But even more amazing about Alabama's appearances is the streak that the "Crimson Tide" began under (Bear) Bryant in 1959 when it appeared in the Liberty Bowl. The "Tide" has appeared in 23 consecutive bowl games, through January 1, 1982.

### Biggest Bowl Score

Centre, of Kentucky, defeated Texas Christian, 63–7, in the 1921 Fort Worth Classic. Among the "Big Four" of bowls (Rose, Orange, Cotton, Sugar), Alabama has the record—61–6 over Syracuse in the 1953 Orange Bowl.

### All-Around Scorer

Major Ogilvie, an Alabama running back, scored touchdowns in major bowls in each of his four seasons—three years at the Sugar Bowl and one at the Cotton Bowl, 1978–81.

### The 180-Minute Player

Bob Reynolds, a tackle for Stanford, played the full 60 minutes in Stanford's 1934 Rose Bowl loss to Columbia. In the next Rose Bowl game, he again went both offense and defense for the full 60 minutes against Alabama, though his team was again defeated. In 1936, appearing for the third straight year in the Rose Bowl, Reynolds once more played the full game—and Stanford won, 7–0, over Southern Methodist's national champions.

### Biggest Crowd in the Press Box

The 1966 historic showdown between Notre Dame and Michigan State had what is believed to be a record media turnout at State's Spartan Stadium: 745.

Stanford's Bob Reynolds saw 180 minutes of action in Rose Bowl contests in the 1930s. The two-way tackle played three consecutive complete games in the post-season event.

## Consecutive Sellout Games

Nebraska, going into the 1982 football season, had sold out 112 straight games, dating back to the 1962 season. Its current capacity for seating is 73,351. Cornhusker fans, being as loyal as they are, once sent 20,000 fans to a game at the University of Hawaii. The team rewarded them with a 61–3 victory.

## First 100,000 Crowd

About 111,000 fans in Chicago's Soldier Field constituted football's first 100,000-plus crowd in 1926, to watch Navy tie Army, 21–21.

## Most 100,000 Crowds

Michigan, with the largest college-owned stadium in the United States (104,700), had a string of 41 straight crowds of more than 100,000 going after the 1981 season.

## Largest Bowl Crowd

The 1973 Rose Bowl game in Pasadena, California, drew 106,869 fans to watch Southern California defeat Ohio State, 42–17.

## Worst Attendance

The worst attendance for a college football game was recorded on November 12, 1955 at Pullman, Washington. The game was between

Washington State and San Jose State. It was played in spite of high winds and a temperature of 0°F. Total paid attendance: 1.

### The Highest Stadium

The highest college in the U.S. is Western State, at Gunnison, Colorado. The school stands 7,735 feet above sea level, and boasts an even higher football stadium—it rises 7,765 feet above sea level.

### Smallest College Currently Playing Football

Northwestern College, in Watertown, Wisconsin, fielded a football team in 1981, though it had only 280 male students.

### Smallest "Big-Time" Team

St. Mary's College, of Moraga, California, had perhaps the most success on the football field for a school with the fewest students enrolled. With only a student body of 150, St. Mary's "Galloping Gaels" had a combined 13–3 record in the 1945 and 1946 regular seasons, despite playing Southern Cal, U.C.L.A. and California. St. Mary's defeated Cal, 20–13, in 1945, and earned a trip to the 1946 Sugar Bowl, where it lost to Oklahoma A&M (now Oklahoma State).

### Only Heisman Winner to Have Stadium Named After Him

Kinnick Stadium, at the University of Iowa, is named after 1939 Heisman Trophy winner Nile Kinnick, who died in World War II.

### Best Halftime Hoax

Though the University of Washington represented the West Coast in the 1961 Rose Bowl game against Minnesota, Cal Tech stole the halftime show—literally stole it. The super-bright engineers from Cal Tech devised a plan, and pulled it off, in which they sneaked into the inner workings of the ultra-sophisticated Washington card section—the 2,232-member student body group that did its cheering by a well-synchronized lifting of colored cards to spell out messages. The engineers did such a good job of substituting their own plan that at halftime, on national television, the message "CALTECH" was unraveled instead of "WASHINGTON," followed by a backward spelling of Washington's nickname (Huskies) and a grand finale in which a Beaver (Cal Tech's mascot) showed up instead of a Huskie.

### Worst Prediction

The 1958 Louisiana State team was picked to finish ninth in the Southeastern Conference. It finished undefeated in all 10 games and won the national championship.

(Above) Western State College in Gunnison, Colorado, has the highest stadium in the world at 7,765 feet above sea level. Not only is football played, but track events can go on simultaneously here, while gymnasts and swimmers compete in the college's nearby "highest altitude" gym and natatorium.

(Below) The wall is the record. Built in 1936–37, it is granite and extends for 3,500 feet to surround the football stadium at St. Cloud State University in Minnesota.

■ Football ■ 113

Army's highest-scoring backfield stars were Glenn Davis (left) and Felix (Doc) Blanchard (right) who teamed up in the mid-1940s to excite football fans everywhere with their rushing. Blanchard, a diving fullback, won the Heisman trophy in 1945 and Davis, a superb open-field runner, won it in 1946. Davis also is tied for the record for most touchdowns (59) in a college career.

### Best Turnaround Season

The 1942 Purdue team had a disastrous 1-8-0 record, scoring only 27 points against the opponents' 179. In 1949, the "Boilermakers" finished 9-0-0. Purdue's cross-state rival, Indiana, nearly duplicated that turnaround—the best in N.C.A.A. history—when it went from 1-8-1 in 1966 to a 9-1-0 Rose Bowl season in 1967.

### Team Scoring

Most points per game by a major-college team in modern times (since the N.C.A.A. began keeping records in 1937) was an average of 56.0 by the 1945 Army team, led by its touchdown tandem Glenn Davis and Felix "Doc" Blanchard.

The most prolific scoring team over a period of time was Michigan's famous "Point-a-Minute" teams of 1901–05. The Wolverines did not quite live up to the billing of 60 points a game, but they were close, with 2,821 in 57 games for a 49.5 scoring average. In 50 of those games, they shut out the opposition. Among the victories were a 128–0 victory over Buffalo in 1901, 119–0 over Michigan State and 107–0 over Iowa in 1902, and 130–0 over West Virginia in 1904. Michigan was tied once during that five-year stretch, then lost its last game in 1905 to Chicago by a 2–0 score.

The most points scored in a game were Georgia Tech's 222 in a shut-out victory over Cumberland on October 7, 1916, in Atlanta, Georgia. Tech was thriving in an era, 1914–17, in which it averaged 45 points a

**Can you find a future President in this picture? Yes, it's Dwight D. Eisenhower (third from the left) when he played at West Point.**

game and only gave up a total of 61. In the record-breaker, Tech scored 32 touchdowns and 30 extra points. Counting rushing yardage and kick returns—Tech did not pass once—it rolled up 968 yards. The closest any teams ever came to matching that score was St. Viator College, in Illinois, which defeated Lane College of Chicago, 205-0—the following week!

The most points scored in the modern era (post 1937) by a major college team is 103, by Wyoming over Northern Colorado, on November 5, 1949. The last major college team to score 100 was Houston, which defeated Tulsa, 100-6, on November 23, 1968, by scoring a record 76 points in the second half. The most points scored by both teams is 124, the result of Oklahoma's 82-42 victory over Colorado on October 4, 1980.

The most points by a losing team is 49, which Washington scored when it lost to California, 54-49, on October 6, 1973.

■ Football ■ 115

The unheralded scoring combination of Bruce Swanson (#12) to Paul Zaeske (#82) for North Park College in Chicago set a pair of small-college (Division III) records when Zaeske caught 8 of Swanson's 10 touchdown passes on October 12, 1968.

In the lower divisions, Portland State scored 105 points against Delaware State in 1980, and Fort Valley State scored 106 against Knoxville in 1969. Davidson scored 55 points in a losing cause (63–55, to Furman), in 1979.

### Best Producers of Passers

Best school for producing great college passers over the years has to be Stanford. The "Cardinals" had the national passing champion six times since such statistics were first kept by the N.C.A.A. in 1937. Those leaders were: Bob Garrett (1953), John Brodie (1956), Dick Norman (1959), Guy Benjamin (1977), Steve Dils (1978) and Turk Schornet (1979). In addition, Stanford produced Frankie Albert, the great passer of the early 1940s; Jim Plunkett, the Heisman-winning quarterback of 1970, and John Elway, its star of the 1980s, who is said to possess the best arm of all the Stanford quarterbacks.

Best coach for producing quarterbacks over the years may be Paul (Bear) Bryant, currently of Alabama. Among his standouts have been

George Blanda and Vito Parilli (at Kentucky), Joe Namath, Ken Stabler, Scott Hunter, Richard Todd and Steve Sloan (at Alabama).

## Pass-Happy Schools

The most pass-happy schools have been Tulsa, which threw 51 passes a game in 1965, and Brigham Young, which gained 409.8 yards a game passing in 1980.

However, a Division I-AA team, Portland State, became the most prolific passing team in the history of college football in 1980. These "Vikings" averaged 434.9 yards a game passing, 52.7 attempts and 32.0 completions a game.

## Most Prolific Recordbreaker

After he finished his four-year career at Portland State University in 1980, Neil Lomax held 90 N.C.A.A. football records and was tied for two other records, mostly on the basis of his passing feats. No other football player, past or present, has been remotely close to holding that many records—in any college sport.

## Short-Handed Team

What could have been a mini-disaster at sea was averted by the Massachusetts Maritime Academy during the 1980 football season. When the season started for the merchant marine training college in Buzzards Bay, Massachusetts, 42 of the veteran players were at sea, required as part of their training. The team lost its first game, but then won four in a row before the veterans got back. When the veterans returned, they began competing for jobs with at least 14 starters—plebes who had started school while they were at sea. The team ended the season with a respectable 6-3-0 record.

## Scoring Streaks

Going into the 1982 football season, Oklahoma had scored in 178 consecutive games.

## Most Questionable Record

The most points ever scored in a college football game by one player is 71, scored by Joe Korshalla of West Liberty State on November 20, 1932. On that day, Korshalla scored 11 touchdowns, none less than 22 yards, made 5 extra points and rolled up an individual total of 504 yards rushing as the West Virginia school defeated Cedarville College of Ohio, 137–0. For the season, Korshalla (or Kershalla as some reports called him) had a total of only 77 points—only 6 more than his record day. Inquiries to West Liberty State even in recent years indicate no en-

**Recognize him? Better known for his baseball skills, Jackie Robinson was a star halfback at U.C.L.A.**

rollment ever of a Joe Korshalla (or Kershalla) that season when he supposedly was a freshman, indicating that he may have been a "ringer." However, West Liberty State did have a *bona fide* graduate, Bob Campiglio, who scored a legitimate 68 points in the previous season, 1931. That is the second-most points on record.

### Best Player Who Never Lived

In 1941, some Wall Street stockbrokers got together and invented a college football team (Plainfield Teachers of New Jersey), fabricated a

Francis "Weenie" Flynn, captain of the 1927 St. Bonaventure University (N.Y.) team, is said to have been the tiniest quarterback in football history. He weighed 117 lbs.

star Chinese halfback (John Chung) and began testing newspapers in the East to see if they could get mention of their imaginary games and Chung's exploits. Beginning with the *Philadelphia Record* and spreading into New York newspaper pages, Plainfield's results were carried that fall, as their made-up school "defeated" Scott, Chesterton, Winona, Randolph Tech, Ingersoll and St. Joseph—none of which existed either. As the gag grew, the stockbrokers provided the newspapers with a telephone number to call and a press agent, who made certain that papers got the scores and Chung's exploits. As the papers got more and more curious, however, and as *Time* magazine got ready to break the story, the stockbrokers sent out one more release, saying that games with Appalachian and Harmony would be canceled because many players had flunked midterm examinations. By then, Chung had "scored" 69 points and Plainfield was "unbeaten," in the sum total of results that got in print that season.

### Best Price for a Big-Time Football Ticket

Northwestern University, winner of only three games in six years, 1976–81, established a family plan for tickets which cost members only

$2 per ticket for the 1981 season. As we go to press, Northwestern still has not won in 29 straight games.

### Oldest Player

Monterey Peninsula College, a California junior college with an enrollment of 2,800, may have had its own George Blanda (the professional player who retired at age 48) in Fritz Von Berg during the 1980 season. Von Berg, a 5-foot-9-inch, 180-pounder, got into a Monterey game as a linebacker and made a tackle—at the age of 50.

### Most-Traveled Team

The 1980 Air Force Academy football team traveled 24,372 miles—just short of the distance around the equator—to play its "away" games. Except for a 226-mile trip from their home in Colorado Springs, Colorado, to play Colorado State in Fort Collins, the Falcons took to the air—to play at Yale, in Connecticut; at West Point, in New York; at Illinois; at Notre Dame, in South Bend, Indiana; at Tulane, in New Orleans; at Washington, in Seattle; at Pacific, in California; and at Hawaii. That meant they played "away" games in five different time zones.

### Longest Road Trip by a Football Team

On November 5, 1979, the University of Miami traveled all the way to Tokyo, Japan, to play (and lose, 40–15) to Notre Dame before 80,000 fans.

### Most All-Americas

Through the 1980 football season, the schools with the most consensus first-team All-America selections were:

| | | | | | |
|---|---|---|---|---|---|
| Yale | 100 | (69 different players) | | | |
| Harvard | 89 | (59) | Ohio State | 46 | (32) |
| Notre Dame | 78 | (67) | Southern Cal | 44 | (38) |
| Michigan | 51 | (41) | Oklahoma | 39 | (34) |
| Penn | 46 | (32) | Army | 37 | (28) |

However, Yale has produced only one consensus All-America since 1937 and Harvard none since 1941. Notre Dame, on the contrary, produced 58 consensus All-Americas in the past four decades.

### All-America Brothers

Twice have three brothers made All-America at the same school. The first trio were the Wistert brothers at Michigan, all of whom were tackles. Francis was honored in 1933, Albert in 1942, Alvin in 1948–49. At Oklahoma, defensive lineman Lucious Selmon was an All-America in

Named All-America in his freshman year, Herschel Walker of Georgia was the outstanding college player in 1980.

1973 and he was followed by his brothers Leroy, a defensive tackle, and Dewey, an offensive guard, in 1975.

### Freshman All-Americas

Herschel Walker of Georgia, a halfback, became, in 1980, the first freshman in the 20th century to be selected consensus All-America, though Frank Steketee of Michigan, in 1918, was named to Walter Camp's All-America team.

### U.S. Presidents Who Played College Football

Eisenhower at West Point.

Kennedy tried out for the team at Harvard.

Nixon at Whittier College, in California.

Ford at Michigan, where he played on a national championship team and later captained the varsity.

Reagan at Eureka College, in Illinois.

### First Televised Football Game

Fordham University, in New York City, was the host to Waynesburg, a Pennsylvania school, in the first football game ever televised—in 1939. Fordham won, 34–7.

# Modern Major-College Football Records
*(1938–1981)*

## SCORING

Most Points, Career
356 Tony Dorsett, Pittsburgh, 1973–76

Most Points, Season
174 Lydell Mitchell, Penn State, 1971

Most Points, Game
43 Jim Brown, Syracuse (vs. Colgate), 1956

Most Touchdowns, Career
59 Glenn Davis, Army (1943–46)

Most Touchdowns, Season
29 Lydell Mitchell, Penn State, 1971

Most Touchdowns, Game
7 Arnold Boykin, Mississippi (vs. Miss. State), 1951

Most Field Goals, Career
60 Obed Ariri, Clemson, 1977–80

Most Field Goals, Season
23 Obed Ariri, Clemson, 1980

Most Field Goals, Game
6 Vince Fusco, Duke (vs. Clemson), 1976
Frank Nestor, W. Virginia (vs. Villanova), 1972
Charley Gogolak, Princeton (vs. Rutgers), 1965

Most Field Goals Made, Consecutive
16 Ish Odonez, Arkansas, 1978–79
Dale Castro, Maryland, 1979

Field Goal, Longest
67 yds. Joe Williams, Wichita State (vs. So. Illinois), 1978
Steve Little, Arkansas (vs. Texas), 1977
Russell Erxleben, Texas (vs. Rice), 1977

Most Points After Touchdown, Consecutive
125 Uwe von Schamann, Oklahoma, 1976–78

## RUSHING

Most Yards Rushing, Career
6,082 Tony Dorsett, Pittsburgh, 1973–76

Most Yards Rushing, Season
2,342 Marcus Allen, Southern Cal, 1981

Most Yards Rushing, Game
356 Eddie Lee Ivery, Georgia Tech (vs. Air Force), 1978

Longest Run from Scrimmage
99 yds. Kelsey Finch, Tennessee (vs. Florida), 1977
Ralph Thompson, West Texas State (vs. Wichita State), 1970
Max Anderson, Arizona State (vs. Wyoming), 1967
Gale Sayers, Kansas (vs. Nebraska), 1963

## PASSING

Most Yards, Career
9,536 Jim McMahon, Brigham Young, 1978–81

Most Yards, Season
4,571 Jim McMahon, Brigham Young, 1980

Most Yards, Game
621 Dave Wilson, Illinois (vs. Ohio State), 1980

Most Attempts, Game
69 Chuck Hixson, Southern Methodist (vs. Ohio State), 1968
Dave Wilson, Illinois (vs. Ohio State), 1980

Most Completions, Game
44 Jim McMahon, Brigham Young (vs. Colorado St.), 1981

Most Touchdown Passes, Career
84 Jim McMahon, Brigham Young, 1978–81

**Most Touchdown Passes, Season**
47 Jim McMahon, Brigham Young, 1980

**Most Touchdown Passes, Game**
9 Dennis Shaw, San Diego State (vs. New Mexico State), 1969

**Longest Pass from Scrimmage**
99 yds. Cris Collinsworth to Derrick Gaffney, Florida (vs. Rice), 1977
Terry Peel to Robert Ford, Houston (vs. San Diego St.), 1972
Terry Peel to Robert Ford, Houston (vs. Syracuse), 1970
Colin Clapton to Eddie Jenkins, Holy Cross (vs. Boston U.), 1970
Bo Burris to Warren McVea, Houston (vs. Washington St.), 1966
Fred Owens to Jack Ford, Portland (vs. St. Mary's), 1947

## RECEIVING

**Most Receptions, Career**
261 Howard Twilley, Tulsa, 1963–65

**Most Receptions, Season**
134 Howard Twilley, Tulsa, 1965

**Most Receptions, Game**
22 Jay Miller, Brigham Young (vs. New Mexico), 1973

**Most Touchdown Passes, Career**
34 Elmo Wright, Houston, 1968–70

**Most Touchdown Passes, Season**
18 Tom Reynolds, San Diego State, 1969

**Most Touchdown Passes, Game**
6 Tim Delaney, San Diego State (vs. New Mexico State), 1969

## INTERCEPTIONS

**Most Interceptions, Career**
29 Al Brosky, Illinois, 1950–52

**Most Interceptions, Season**
14 Al Worley, Washington, 1968

**Most Interceptions, Game**
5 Dan Rebech, Miami, Ohio (vs. Western Michigan), 1972
Byron Beaver, Houston (vs. Baylor), 1962
Walt Pastuszak, Brown (vs. Rhode Island), 1949
Lee Cook, Oklahoma St. (vs. Detroit), 1942

## PUNTING

Best Average, Career (minimum: 75 punts)
46.9 yds. Marv Bateman, Utah, 1970–71

Best Average, Season (minimum: 30 punts)
49.8 yds. Reggie Roby, Iowa, 1981

# ALL SPORTS

### Largest Athletic Population

The record for having the most intercollegiate sports' teams belongs to New York's Cornell University. On the campus (or in nearby refreshment halls) there are members of 40 different teams, of which 22 are men's teams and 18 are women's.

### A 24-Letterman

Elmer Oliphant lived in an era when colleges encouraged their athletes to participate in a sport a season. At Purdue, from 1911-13, Oliphant won nine letters in football, baseball, basketball and track. Then, in 1914, he moved on to West Point, and because of wartime rules he was allowed to continue to participate on the varsity teams. In his four years there, he earned more letters in football, basketball and baseball—captaining each team—and added letters in track, hockey and swimming. That gave him 15 more letters, for a total of 24. Football was considered Oliphant's best sport. He once kicked a crucial field goal despite a broken ankle, made 13 of 13 extra points in one game in which he scored a total of 43 points, and was All-America at West Point.

### Athletic-Academic Combinations

Dartmouth College must hold the record for most Phi Beta Kappas on a national championship team. Its 1925 varsity, which was undefeated, had 22 of them, plus a millionaire industrialist as a coach in Jesse Hawley.

### Athletic-Leadership Combinations

West Point in 1913-14 had some pretty good football players who lost only one game in those two years. But the players became even more impressive after they left school. Omar Bradley, Dwight D. Eisenhower, Robert Neyland, Vernon E. Prichard, Leland S. Hobbs, W. W. Hess Jr. and Roscoe Woodruff were just some of the cadets from those teams who later became generals in the United States Army. Neyland also became one of football's more famous coaches—at Tennessee. West Point's graduating class of 1915, of which many football stars were members, appropriately is referred to at West Point as "the Class the Stars Fell On."

### College Athletes Who Starred in Movies

Johnny Weissmuller, Illinois swimmer, became "Tarzan." So did Clarence "Buster" Crabbe of Southern Cal.

"Crazy Legs" Hirsch was a college star at Wisconsin and Michigan before setting a pro record for catching touchdown passes.

Johnny Mack Brown, Alabama Rose Bowl star, who had a long run of Westerns.

Elroy (Crazy Legs) Hirsch, who played for both Wisconsin and Michigan football teams and other sports, who played himself in the movie "Crazylegs".

John Wayne, Southern Cal (?) football player.

Burt Reynolds, Florida State football player.

Ron Ely, Southern Cal football player, who became a later "Tarzan."

Bernie Casey, Bowling Green football and track star.

Kirk Douglas was a top class wrestler at college.

Jimmy Brown, Syracuse All-America, who starred in the movie "The Dirty Dozen."

Mike Warren, U.C.L.A. basketball player stars in TV's "Hill Street Blues."

O. J. Simpson, Southern Cal football star, played in several movies as well as Hertz rental ads on TV.

## First Conferences

Seven southern colleges met on December 2, 1894, to form the Southern Intercollegiate Athletic Conference, which is now more commonly known as the Southern Conference.

Only 18 days later, seven midwestern schools met to discuss the forming of the Intercollegiate Conference of Faculty Representatives, now known as the Big Ten.

## All-Sports Championship

For winning team titles in N.C.A.A. championship meets, no one is close to Southern Cal, which has won 63. The Trojans have won in baseball, gymnastics, tennis, indoor track, outdoor track and volleyball. The Trojans have also produced the most individual champions (243), which is why the school is believed to have produced more Olympians than any other college in America. Next to Southern Cal in team titles are U.C.L.A. (39), Oklahoma State (35), Michigan (27) and Yale (25). Behind Southern Cal in individual titles are Michigan (179), Ohio State (161), Oklahoma State (112) and Yale (104).

## Best Professional Prospect

Dave Winfield of the University of Minnesota had to be the most sought-after athlete by the professionals. He is believed to be the only athlete drafted by the pros in baseball, basketball and football, even though he did not play the latter sport at Minnesota. Winfield, the most valuable player in the 1973 College World Series, eventually signed to play baseball and became a multi-millionaire in the sport with the New York Yankees.

## All-Around Athlete

In the 1912 Olympics Jim Thorpe, football star and all-around athlete, was the hero of the Games, winning both the pentathlon and decathlon. His medals, however, were later taken away when the A.A.U. discovered he had accepted pay for playing baseball, but in 1973, some 20 years after his death, he was reinstated as an amateur.

## Broderick Awards

The Broderick Awards are given by the Association for Intercollegiate Athletics for Women (A.I.A.W.) to the outstanding collegiate women athletes of the year in each of the championship sports. An overall outstanding athlete is then selected from among the award winners, and presented with the Broderick Cup.

Winners of the Broderick Cup have been:

1976–77  Lusia Harris Stewart, Delta State University (Basketball)
1977–78  Ann Meyers, U.C.L.A. (Basketball)
1978–79  Nancy Lieberman, Old Dominion University (Basketball)
1979–80  Julie Shea, North Carolina State (Track and Field)

Winners of the Broderick Awards were:

**1976-77**

| | |
|---|---|
| Badminton | Denise Corlett, U.C.L.A. |
| Basketball | Lusia Harris Stewart, Delta State |
| Cross Country | Julie Brown, Cal State—Northridge |
| Field Hockey | Karen Shelton, West Chester State |
| Golf | Beth Daniel, Furman |
| Gymnastics | Ann Carr, Penn State |
| | Connie Jo Israel, Clarion State |
| Skiing | Toril Forland, Utah |
| Softball | Audie Kujala, Delaware |
| Swimming & Diving | Melissa Belote, Arizona State |
| Tennis | Kathy Mueller, Trenton State |
| Track and Field | Julie Brown, Cal State—Northridge |
| | Evelyn Ashford, U.C.L.A. |
| Volleyball | Flora Hyman, Houston |

**1977-78**

| | |
|---|---|
| Badminton | Carrie Morrison, Arizona State |
| Basketball | Ann Meyers, U.C.L.A. |
| Cross Country | Kathy Mills, Penn State |
| Field Hockey | Karen Shelton, West Chester State |
| Golf | Debbie Petrizzi, Texas |
| Gymnastics | Ann Carr, Penn State |
| Skiing | Toril Forland, Utah |
| Softball | Kathy Arendsen, Texas Woman's Univ. |

When Beth Daniel, now a top-money winner on the pro golf tour, was a student at Furman College (Greenville, South Carolina) in 1976-77, she won a Broderick Award.

| | |
|---|---|
| Swimming & Diving | Renee Laravie, Florida |
| Tennis | Jeanne DuVall, U.C.L.A. |
| Track and Field | Kathy Mills, Penn State |
| Volleyball | Debbie Green, Southern Cal |

**1978-79**

| | |
|---|---|
| Badminton | Ann French, Wisconsin |
| Basketball | Nancy Lieberman, Old Dominion |
| Cross Country | Kathy Mills, Penn State |
| Field Hockey | Karen Shelton, West Chester State |
| Golf | Kyle O'Brien, Southern Methodist |
| Gymnastics | Kolleen Casey, Southwest Missouri State |
| Skiing | Sara McNealus, Middlebury |
| Softball | Kathy Arendsen, Texas Woman's Univ. |
| Swimming & Diving | Joan Pennington, Texas |
| Synchronized Swimming | Ruth Pickett, Michigan |
| Tennis | Kathy Jordan, Stanford |
| Track and Field | Jodi Anderson, Cal State—Northridge |
| Volleyball | Annette Cottle, Utah State |

**1979-80**

| | |
|---|---|
| Badminton | Janet Wentworth, Northern Illinois |
| Basketball | Nancy Lieberman, Old Dominion |
| Cross Country | Joan Benoit, Bowdoin |
| Field Hockey | Brenda Becker, West Chester State |
| Golf | Patty Sheehan, San Jose State |
| Gymnastics | Ann Carr, Penn State |
| Skiing | Lindy Cochran, Vermont |
| Softball | Kathy Arendsen, Cal State—Chico |
| Swimming & Diving | Jill Sterkel, Texas |
| Synchronized Swimming | Ruth Pickett, Michigan |
| Tennis | Wendy White, Rollins |
| Track and Field | Julie Shea, North Carolina State |
| Volleyball | Ann Meyer, Dayton |

Catch, girls! This is basketball as played at Barnard College in 1900, only 8 years after it was invented.

# BASKETBALL

### Basketball on Campus

Basketball caught on like wildfire soon after it was invented in January 1892, and proceeded to invade most college campuses. Girls could play as well as boys, and female students of Barnard College around the turn of the century were said to take the sport quite seriously.

### Best Combination Scorer-Rebounder

Bill Mlkvy, who had the nickname "Owl without a Vowel" when he played for Temple University in the early 1950s, was the nation's leading scorer (29.2 points a game) and the second-leading rebounder (18.9 a game) in the 1950–51 season. No one has ever won both crowns nor has anyone come as close as Mlkvy. Lewis Lloyd of Drake University, however, was second in both categories during the 1979–80 season.

### Top Field-Goal Shooter

Steve Johnson, from Oregon State, made 74.6 percent of his field goals in the 1980-81 season.

### Twice M.V.P. in N.C.A.A. Tournaments

Players who have been named twice to the Most Valuable Player honor in the N.C.A.A. tournament are:

Invented by Dr. James Naismith in December 1891, in Springfield, Massachusetts, where he was director of the Y.M.C.A. Training School, part of Springfield College, basketball was first played before spectators in January 1892.

Bob Kurland, Oklahoma A&M (now Oklahoma State); Alex Groza, Kentucky; Jerry Lucas, Ohio State; Lew Alcindor, U.C.L.A.; and Bill Walton, U.C.L.A.

### Best Season Attendance

The University of Kentucky broke the collegiate attendance record for the fifth year in a row during the 1980–81 season when it averaged 23,666 fans a game at its Rupp Arena.

### One-Game Attendance

The University of Houston and U.C.L.A. drew a crowd of 52,693 to their showdown between Houston's Elvin Hayes and U.C.L.A.'s Lew Alcindor (later called Kareem Abdul-Jabbar) on January 20, 1968. No other schools have come within 15,000 of that record-breaking crowd at the Houston Astrodome.

### Longest Name

Ajoritsedabi Oreghoyeyere Memaridieyin Okorodudu, who played for Bucknell University in the early 1980s season. In the program, his 45 letters were cut down considerably, to Deb Okorodudu.

### Free-Throw Shooting

Russell Thompson, of Birmingham Southern College, in Alabama, never made a shot from the floor in his team's 55–46 victory over Florence State in January, 1971. Yet he went to the free-throw line 28 times, made 25 of them, and had a pretty good night as a result. The reason for Thompson getting all his points from the line was that Birmingham Southern was ordered by its coach to play a slowdown game and Thompson, being the team's playmaking guard, was fouled often.

Three-time All-America center Lew Alcindor (#33) was as dominant a basketball figure at U.C.L.A. as he has been as a pro under the name of Kareem Abdul-Jabbar.

■ Basketball ■ 131

Highest scoring player (4,061 points) in college basketball history was Pearl Moore (left) of Francis Marion College (Florence, South Carolina). She scored 42 points in her final game in 1979 to surpass the previous career record by just 16 points. Her one-game high was 60 points.

## Highest Scoring Collegian

Only two collegians have ever scored more than 4,000 points in their college careers, and the top-scoring one was Pearl Moore, a member of the Francis Marion College women's team. Miss Moore, a 5-foot-7-inch guard and forward, surpassed the record of 4,045 by Travis Grant, a Kentucky State player, when she scored 42 points in her final game in 1979, to bring her career total to 4,061. She averaged 30.1 points a game throughout her career, which began with eight games at Anderson Junior College, in South Carolina, and the rest at Francis Marion, in her home town of Florence, Southern Carolina. Her personal best was 60 points in one game, against Eastern Washington University, in 1978.

## Free-Throw Accuracy by a Team

The University of California-Irvine set a major-college record for perfect free-throw shooting when its players made all 34 of their shots in a game against Pacific in February, 1981.

## 2,000-Point Scorers

St. Bonaventure is the only Division I school that can boast four of its former stars who have made as many as 2,000 points in a season. The players are Tom Stith, Bob Lanier, Greg Sanders and Earl Belcher.

## Rained-Out Game

When the State Fair Arena, where Oklahoma City University plays its home games, leaked too much water in January, 1980, O.C.U. had to postpone its scheduled basketball game with University of Nevada-Las Vegas, making it perhaps college basketball's first rained-out game.

## High-Five Inventors

The "high five", a hand-slapping show of jubilation high over the head, became the well-known mark of success for all sorts of teammates, pro and amateur, in the 1980s. Its inventor is believed to be Derek Smith, who popularized it in the 1979-80 season while playing for the University of Louisville's national championship basketball team.

## First 3-Point Basket

For the 1980-81 basketball season, the Southern Conference was designated to experiment with the rule that allows for 3 points for a field goal beyond a certain distance (in this case, a radius of 22 feet from the basket). The first player to make a 3-pointer was Ronnie Carr, a 6-foot-3-inch guard from Western Carolina University.

Bevo Francis' scoring ability attracted so many spectators to the games he played in for little Rio Grande College of Ohio, that he saved the college from bankruptcy in 1952–53. His high was 116 points in a game (113 officially) and he averaged 46.5 points per game one season.

134 ■ College Records ■

### Greatest Scorer

Nobody in college basketball has ever scored more than Clarence (Bevo) Francis, who played for little Rio (pronounced Ryo) Grande College, of Ohio. Francis was with the team for only two seasons—1952–53 and 1953–54. As a freshman, he once scored 116 points against a two-year school, but that record never went in the book because it was against a junior college. But the next season, Francis scored 113 in a game that did count, against Hillsdale College. He also has the best average for a season—46.5 points. In his career, albeit only two seasons, he scored over 50 points 14 times. He once shot a record 71 times in a game—against Alliance—and made 38 baskets. He made 37 free throws in his 113-point game, another record.

### Major College Scoring

The most points in a game is 100, by Frank Selvy of Furman, against Newberry College on February 13, 1954. Pete Maravich, Louisiana State, had the best scoring average (44.5 points a game, 1969–70 season) and the best career average (44.2, 1967–70).

Selvy made 41 field goals in his 100-point game, the most ever by a collegian.

### Most Points in a Game, Team

The University of Nevada-Las Vegas scored 164 points in beating the University of Hawaii-Hilo on February 19, 1976. Hilo scored 111.

### Most Points by a Losing Team

Utah scored 120 points against St. Joseph's of Pennsylvania on March 25, 1961, but lost by seven points after four overtimes.

### 100-Point Games

Nevada-Las Vegas scored at least 100 points in 23 games in the 1975–76 season and repeated the feat a season later.

### Widest Victory Margin

Louisiana State defeated Southwestern of Tennessee, 124–33, on December 8, 1952, for a 91-point margin.

### Pro-Oriented

The 1960 Ohio State starting lineup had to be the most successful five when it came to pro careers. All five starters—Jerry Lucas, John Havlicek, Mel Nowell, Joe Roberts and Larry Siegfried not only made it to the pros, but averaged at least 10 points a game during one of their seasons in the National Basketball Association.

Ronnie and Donnie Creamer of Williamston, South Carolina, are identical twins who stand more than 6 feet 10½ inches high. Of course, they played basketball for Winthrop College.

## All-Around Player

In the 1980-81 season, Kevin Magee, University of California-Irvine, became the only major college player to rank in the top four nationally in scoring, rebounding and field-goal percentage. He averaged 27.5 points a game, had 12.5 rebounds a game and shot 67.1 percent from the floor. Considering that only 13 other players have ranked that highly in as many as two categories, it shows how impressive the 6-foot-8-inch Magee was.

Ohio State's Jerry Lucas had the best double, as he was No. 1 in both rebounding and field-goal percentage in both 1960-61 and 1961-62.

## Winningest Coaches

Adolph Rupp's teams, all at the University of Kentucky (1931-72) won 874 games. Rupp's major-college won-loss percentage was 82.1, second only to Clair Bee, the coach at Rider (1929-31) and Long Island University (1932-45 and 1946-51). A small-college coach, John Retton of Fairmont (W. Va.) State has an 84.7 percent success record for 18 seasons going into the 1981-82 campaign.

## Unbeatens

In basketball's modern era, defined as the period beginning in 1938 when the center jump was eliminated, only 13 teams have gone undefeated through the regular season and tournament play. Those teams were: Long Island University (1939), Seton Hall (1940), Army (1944), Columbia (1951), Kentucky (1954), San Francisco (1956), North Carolina (1957), U.C.L.A. (1964, 1967, 1972 and 1973), North Carolina State (1973) and Indiana (1976).

## Winning Seasons

The University of Louisville has had 37 consecutive winning seasons, going into the 1981-82 season. Counting .500 (or break-even) seasons, the University of Kentucky has gone 54 straight seasons without a losing team.

## Home-Court Edge

The Kentucky Wildcats won 129 consecutive games at home, from January 4, 1943, until January 8, 1955, when they were beaten by Georgia Tech, 59-58.

## Longest Winning Streak

U.C.L.A. won 88 games in a row, from January 30, 1971, until January 17, 1974, when the Bruins were beaten by Notre Dame, 71-70.

In major-college basketball, Pete Maravich of Louisiana State holds a fistful of scoring records, including the best scoring average—44.5 points per game in 1970. When he joined the pros later that year, the Atlanta Hawks gave him the most lucrative contract up to that time—$1,500,000 for five years.

## Modern Major-College Basketball Records
### (1938-1981)
### SCORING

Most Points, Game
  100  Frank Selvy, Furman vs. Newberry, Feb. 13, 1954

Most Points, Season
  1,381  Pete Maravich, Louisiana State, 1970

Most Points, Career
  3,667  Pete Maravich, Louisiana State, 1968-70

### FIELD GOALS

Most Field Goals, Game
  41  Frank Selvy, Furman vs. Newberry, Feb. 13, 1954 (66 att.)

Most Field Goals, Season
  522  Pete Maravich, Louisiana State, 1970 (1,168 att.)

Most Field Goals, Career
  1,387  Pete Maravich, Louisiana State, 1968-70 (3,166 att.)

Most Consecutive Field Goals, Season
  25  Ray Voelkel, American, 1978 (during 9 games)

Most Field Goal Attempts, Game
  71  Jay Handlan, Washington & Lee vs. Furman, Feb. 17, 1951 (made 30)

Most Field Goal Attempts, Season
1,168  Pete Maravich, Louisiana State, 1970 (made 522)

Most Field Goal Attempts, Career
3,166  Pete Maravich, Louisiana State, 1968-70 (made 1,387)

Highest Field Goal Percentage, Season (qualifiers)
74.6%  Steve Johnson, Oregon State, 1981 (235 of 315)

Highest Field Goal Percentage, Career (min. 600 scored)
67.8%  Steve Johnson, Oregon State, 1977-81 (828 of 1,222)

### FREE THROWS

Most Free Throws, Game
30  Pete Maravich, Louisiana State vs. Oregon State, Dec. 22, 1969 (31 att.)

Most Free Throws, Season
355  Frank Selvy, Furman, 1954 (444 att.)

Most Free Throws, Career
905  Dickie Hemric, Wake Forest, 1952-55 (1,359 att.)

Most Consecutive Free Throws, Game
24  Arlen Clark, Oklahoma State vs. Colorado, Mar. 7, 1959 (24 of 24)

# BICYCLING

## Size of Other Sports

The University of California at Santa Barbara takes special care of students on bikes—all 12,000 of them! The campus features five miles of bikeways and three bike underpasses. This intricate system of small roadways turns out to be the most complete bikeway system in the U.S.

# BASEBALL

## Most National Collegiate Baseball Titles

Southern Cal has won 11 N.C.A.A. titles since the College World Series was inaugurated in 1947. In 10 of those World Series, the Trojan coach was Ron Dedeaux.

In Division II of the N.C.A.A., Florida Southern has won a record five titles since the first divisional playoffs in 1968.

Most Consecutive Free Throws, Season
60  Bob Lloyd, Rutgers, 1967

Most Free Throw Attempts, Game
36  Ed Tooley, Brown vs. Amherst, Dec. 4, 1954 (made 23)

Most Free Throw Attempts, Career
1,359  Dickie Hemric, Wake Forest, 1952-55 (made 905)

Highest Free Throw Percentage, Season
94.4%  Carlos Gibson, Marshall, 1978 (84 of 89)

Highest Free Throw Percentage, Career
88.5%  Ron Perry, Holy Cross, 1976-80 (680 of 768)

### REBOUNDS

Most Rebounds, Game
51  Bill Chambers, William & Mary vs. Virginia, Feb. 14, 1953

Most Rebounds, Season
734  Walt Dukes, Seton Hall, 1953

Most Rebounds, Career
2,201  Tom Gola, LaSalle, 1952-55

Highest Average Rebounds per Game, Season
25.6  Charlie Slack, Marshall, 1955 (538 in 21 games)

Highest Average Rebounds per Game, Career (min. 800)
22.7  Artis Gilmore, Jacksonville, 1970-71 (1,224 in 54 games)

In the last few decades, more baseball professionals have come direct from college ball fields. To some extent, this was because more athletes were attending college. For example, Arizona State won the collegiate national championship in 1964, and who were some of the players? Sal Bando was the most valuable player, and his teammates were Reggie Jackson (above) and Rick Monday. The three ended up on the championship Oakland A's within a few years.

### Best Batting Average in Playoffs

Notre Dame's Jim Morris hit .714 (10 for 14) in the 1957 College World Series.

### Most Home Runs in College World Series Game

Terry Brumfield of Southern Illinois hit three home runs in a game off Ball State University, 1969.

### Most Strikeouts in College Playoff Game

Steve Arlin of Ohio State struck out 20 Washington State batters in a 15-inning game in 1965. That record was matched by a Division II pitcher, Ted Barnicle of Jacksonville State against Southeastern Louisiana in a 9-inning game in 1975. But Ed Bane of Arizona State may have had the best strikeout pitch of all in post-season play. He struck out 17 Oklahoma batters in a game in 1972 and 19 Denver batters in 1973.

### Best Promoter in College Baseball

Ron Fraser, coach at the University of Miami since 1963, sold 2,300 season tickets to Hurricane games for the 1981 season, a collegiate record by more than 700. His 1981 team had consecutive crowds of 5,661, 6,688 and 4,248 and boosted its attendance over 100,000—only the third team other than Arizona and Arizona State to achieve that figure in a day when some schools are dropping baseball to save money. Among Fraser's promotions: Bathing Beauty Night, Tax Night (everyone got assistance in filling out forms) and a Money Scramble, where two fans were selected to keep as much of the $5,000 that was scattered about the field as they could gather within an allotted time.

One of the greatest college players ever was "Columbia Lou" Gehrig, who went right to the Yankees after graduation. When Columbia baseball games were played at South Field, Gehrig hit a pitched ball from home plate at 114th Street and Amsterdam Avenue almost to 116th Street and Broadway, where it crashed through a window of the Journalism Building, a distance estimated at more than 600 feet on the fly.

## CROSS-COUNTRY

### Winningest Cross-Country Team

Michigan State has won eight team titles since the N.C.A.A. meet was begun in 1938. However, the University of Texas, El Paso, which has won six times, took the championship title five times from 1975-80.

### Individual Cross-Country Champions

Washington State has produced more individual champions in the N.C.A.A. meet than any other school, with six. Gerry Lindgren (1966-67-69) and Henry Rono (1976-77-79) each won three of those titles for Washington State. The only other individual to win three titles was Steve Prefontaine of Oregon (1970-71-73).

In cross-country racing, Gerry Lindgren of Washington State (shown here in practice) won three titles for his college—in 1966, 1967 and 1969.

## FENCING

### Most Fencing Champions

Since the N.C.A.A. fencing championships were first held in 1941, New York University has won 12 team titles and has had 23 individual champions, far more than any other school in both categories.

## GOLF

### Most Golf Team Champions

The forerunner to the N.C.A.A. golf championships, the National Collegiate Golf Championships, conducted by the Intercollegiate Golf Association of America, dates back to 1897. Including that championship and the N.C.A.A.'s official tournament, Yale has won 21 team titles and produced 13 individual champions.

### Greatest College Golfer

Ben Crenshaw, a current professional star, undoubtedly had the best intercollegiate career. As the later of the University of Texas teams in the early 1970s, he won three individual N.C.A.A. titles (1971-72-73, though sharing low-score honors in 1972 with Tom Kite, his teammate).

He also holds the record for the lowest 72-hole score in N.C.A.A. championship play—a 272 (15 under par) in 1971.

## Most Famous Golf Coach

Dave Williams, University of Houston, has produced 13 N.C.A.A. team titles since 1956, as well as four teams that were runners-up. Seven of his golfers have had the low-score honors in N.C.A.A. championship tournaments.

## Famous Golfing Alumni

Arnold Palmer, Wake Forest; Jack Nicklaus, Ohio State; Phil Rodgers, Houston; Kermit Zarley, Houston; Hale Irwin, Colorado; Curtis Strange, Wake Forest; John Mahaffey, Houston.

Jack Nicklaus (left) came right out of Ohio State to dominate the professional golf tour in 1962. Arnold Palmer, the leading money winner before Nicklaus, made Wake Forest, his alma mater, known throughout the golfing world.

■ Cross-Country—Fencing—Golf ■ 143

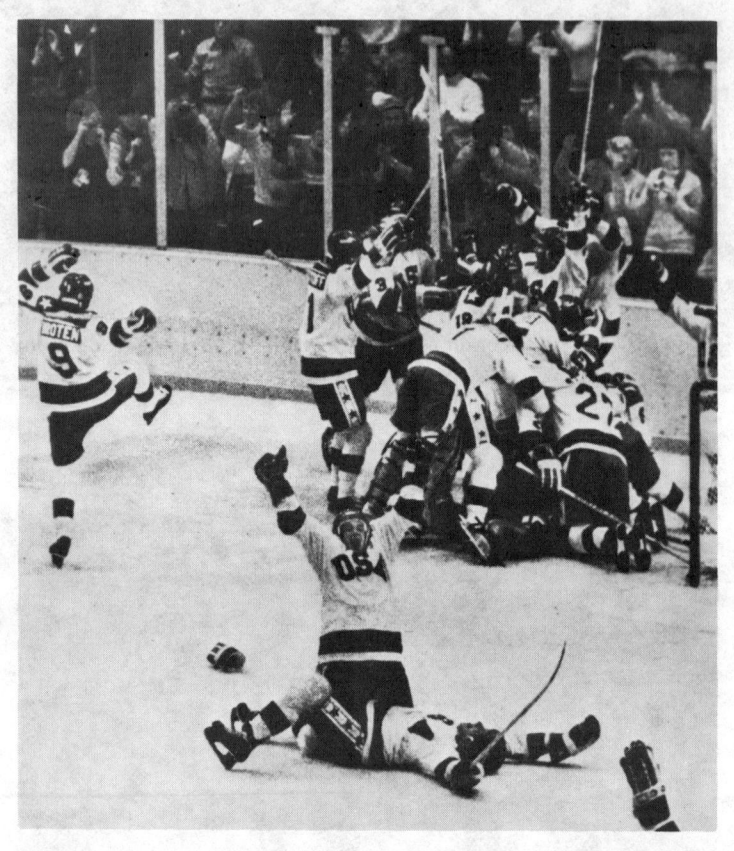

Winning the gold medal in the 1980 Olympics was one of the high points of amateur hockey in the United States. Coached by Herb Brooks, whose teams at the University of Minnesota had captured 3 national championships, the Olympic team was comprised of collegiate players. Currently, more N.H.L. players are coming from the college ranks than ever before.

# GYM

### Most National Gym Team Titles

Penn State has won nine N.C.A.A. meets, one more than Illinois, through the 1981 championships. Illinois has a slight edge over Penn State in all-time individual champions, 39–34.

### Winningest Athletes in National Gym Meets

Joe Gaillombardo of Illinois won a record seven individual N.C.A.A. titles from 1938–40. Jean Cronstedt of Penn State (1954) and Robert Lynn of Southern Cal (1962) were the only men to win four individual titles in one meet.

### Rope Climb

The Guinness world record for a 20-foot rope climb (hands only) is 2.8 seconds, set by Don Perry in 1954. At the time, the rope climb was an official intercollegiate gymnastics event, and Perry was a U.C.L.A. student.

## HOCKEY

### Most Hockey Championships Won

Since the N.C.A.A. tournament began in 1948, Michigan has won the most tournaments (seven), having taken six of the first nine. Michigan and Boston University, with 13 appearances each, have played in the tournament the most times.

### Most Goals in N.C.A.A. Tournament Game

Michigan defeated Boston University, 14–2, in 1953, and Minnesota defeated Boston College, 14–1, in 1954, to set the record for most goals in a tournament game. The record for individuals is 5, shared by Carl Lawrence of Colorado College and Gil Burford of Michigan, both of whom had Boston College as their opponent in 1950 when they achieved their feats.

### Most Points in N.C.A.A. Tournament Game

Boston University scored 25 points on 10 goals in beating Harvard, 10–5, in 1975. The individual record is 7 points, scored by John Mayasich of Minnesota in 1954 (against Boston College).

### Most Points in a Hockey Tournament

Aaron Broten of Minnesota had 13 points in the 1981 tournament, which was played in an eight-team format (as opposed to the former four-team playoff) for the first time.

### Best Team Record

Cornell, winner of the 1966 national hockey championship, had a 27-1-1 record.

### American Hockey Olympians

The University of Minnesota has produced more players for the United States Olympic teams than any other school. On the winning 1980 team alone, the Gophers had 9 of the 20 places on the roster.

### Winningest Coaches

Going into the 1981-82 season, only two coaches had ever won more than 500 games. John Kelley of Boston College became the first, bringing his total to 501 in 1971-72. John MacInnes surpassed that figure in 1980, coaching at Michigan Tech, in Houghton, Michigan, and brought that total up to 532 after the 1980-81 season.

## LACROSSE

### Best Lacrosse School

Johns Hopkins has won four N.C.A.A. championships and has been the No. 1 or No. 2 team in eight of the 11 years of the tournament.

### Scoring in Lacrosse

Four players have each scored seven goals in an N.C.A.A. tournament game. They are: Tom Cafaro (Army, 1971); Franz Wittlesberger (John Hopkins, 1974); Ed Mullen (Maryland, 1976) and Mike French (Cornell, 1976). Eamon McEnearney (Cornell, 1977) holds the record for most points in a tournament—25 in three games.

## ROWING

### First Intercollegiate Competition

Yale, which began rowing in 1843, and Harvard, which took up the sport in 1845, were the first American schools to participate in intercollegiate competition in *any* sport when their crews met in the summer of 1852.

## SKIING

### Most Ski Championships

The University of Denver has won 14 N.C.A.A. skiing team titles since 1954. Thirteen of those teams were coached by Willy Schaeffler, who also had five runner-up teams. Chiharu Igaya, Dartmouth, won six international N.C.A.A. titles from 1955-57.

Hockey coach John MacInnes of Michigan Tech proudly displays the award he received for his teams winning a total of 532 games.

When it comes to lacrosse (and medical colleges) Johns Hopkins has been the leader. Here Hopkins is battling against nearby University of Maryland.

■ Hockey—Lacrosse—Rowing—Skiing ■

The University of California crew, representing the U.S.A. in the 1932 Olympics at Los Angeles, did not have far to go in winning the 8-oared shell race, but it won by barely "a nose" over Italy, Canada and Great Britain.

# SOCCER

### Most Powerful Soccer Team

St. Louis University has played in all 22 N.C.A.A. soccer tournaments and has won 10 titles.

### Soccer Scoring

Thompson Usiyan, Appalachian State, scored a record seven goals against George Washington University in a 1978 N.C.A.A. tournament game.

### Longest Overtime Soccer Game

Bridgeport University and West Chester State played 10 overtimes and a total of 153 minutes 24 seconds before Bridgeport won, 2–1.

A game lasted 265 minutes at Pasadena, California, in November 1976, between Simon Fraser University and Quincy College.

Winner of 10 N.C.A.A. titles is John Naber of Southern Cal, 1974-77. He went on to win 4 gold medals in the 1976 Olympics, setting world records in the 100 and 200 meter backstroke.

## SWIMMING

### Championship Swimming Teams

Ohio State (11), Michigan (10) and Southern Cal (9) have won 30 of the first 45 N.C.A.A. team titles in swimming. Ohio State and Michigan have each had 112 individual winners in the meet.

### Individual Swimming Titles

John Naber, a Southern Cal swimmer, won 10 titles in the N.C.A.A. meet, from 1974-77. He also swam on five winning relay teams and won both backstroke events all four years that he swam for U.S.C.

### Staying Afloat

The duration record for treading water was set at California State College-Chico by Kenton D. Smith, August 28-31, 1980. He stayed afloat in a vertical position in an 8-foot square without touching anything (not even the lane markers) for 72 hours 13 seconds.

Diana Nyad, while studying for a Ph.D. at N.Y.U., in 1974 attempted a number of marathon swims. Then in 1975, she entered the East River off 89th Street for a swim around Manhattan Island, New York, through polluted waters and through a harbor filled with ocean-going ships and ferryboats, to set a record of 7 hours 57 minutes for the feat.

### College Student Attempts Hellespont Swim

After winning a 4-year scholarship to U.C.L.A., Jack Wheeler of Glendale, California, in November 1960 (late in the year for a swim), flew after an 8 a.m. class on Friday to Turkey, entered the sea when the water was only 59°F. and starting at midnight, swam for 3 hours, but had to be pulled from the icy water, his leg cramped. He slept for 3 hours, then flew back to Los Angeles, arriving in time for his Monday morning classes.

# TENNIS

### Tennis Team Championships

U.C.L.A. has won 13 team titles in the N.C.A.A. tennis championships that began in 1946. That's one more than Southern Cal won. Harvard has had the most singles champions (16) and is tied with Southern Cal (at 17) for the most doubles champions.

### Veteran Tennis Team

County College of Morris, in Randolph, New Jersey, boasted one of college sport's most veteran teams ever when it sent its tennis team to the courts in 1980. Among the members of the six-woman traveling team: 36-year-old Carol O'Donnell, the No. 1 singles player; 40-year-old Mary Harring, the No. 3 singles player; and 34-year-old Debbie Masefield, the No. 4 singles player. All were married and among them had five children. They helped the college win 21 straight dual matches.

The California colleges have produced champion tennis players since the 1940s, and most of the collegians have gone on to successful careers in amateur and professional play. Dennis Ralston won the N.C.A.A. singles title for Southern Cal in 1963 and 1964.

Continuing California colleges' dominance of the tennis courts, it was Arthur Ashe (above) of U.C.L.A. who took over from Ralston. And then in 1966, Charles Pasarell of U.C.L.A. (left) was the winner.

# TRACK AND FIELD

## Most Championship Track Teams—Outdoors

Since the first N.C.A.A. meet in 1921, Southern Cal has won 26 team titles. No other team has won more than five. In the championship meets, Southern Cal produced 92 individual champions, which is more than twice that of the runner-up, U.C.L.A.

## Best Individual Performer in N.C.A.A. Meet

Only one athlete has ever won four individual titles in one championship meet, and that man, Jesse Owens while at Ohio State, did it twice—in 1935 as a sophomore and 1936 as a junior. Each time, Owens won the 100-yard dash, 220-yard dash, 220-yard low hurdles and the long jump. Owens did not compete in 1937 because he turned professional after the 1936 Olympics. Freshmen were not eligible to compete in that era.

## Repeat Champions

Steve Prefontaine, a three-mile runner for Oregon, did compete as a freshman and won his event that year (1970) and for the next three years, becoming the first four-time champion in one event. Scott Neilson, University of Washington hammer thrower, is the only other athlete to match the four-time feat, winning his event from 1976–79.

## Most Championship Track Teams—Indoors

The University of Texas–El Paso, has won six N.C.A.A. indoor titles, though Villanova University has a slight 28–27 edge over U.T.E.P. in individual champions.

## Greatest One-Day Performance

The greatest one-day performance in college track and field—or in any level of track and field, or for that matter in the history of any sport—was Jesse Owens's four-world-record day in the Big Ten championships when he was running for Ohio State at Ann Arbor, Michigan, on May 25, 1935. Within a 45-minute span that day, Owens tied the world record in the 100-yard dash, broke the record in the 220-yard dash, smashed the record in the 220-yard hurdles and set a record in the long jump (26 feet 8¼ inches) that would last for 25 years. In addition, his 220-yard records were ratified as 220-meter marks as well, giving Owens six world records that day.

### Fastest Preparation for Olympics

Otis Davis was a 26-year-old Oregon basketball player when the track coach asked him to try out for the team in 1958. He ran mostly shorter sprints, used up his eligibility before his senior year, and got to compete in only about ten 440-yard events (or its 400-meter Olympic equivalent) before the 1960 Olympics. At the Games in Rome, he ran the 400 meters in a world-record 44.9 seconds and won the gold medal.

### Honors

Julie Shea, a distance runner for North Carolina State, became the first woman to be named the outstanding athlete (regardless of sex) in a major conference when she was selected by a predominantly male sportswriters association in 1980 as the top athlete in the basketball-strong Atlantic Coast Conference. In 1981, she became only the third athlete to be so-honored twice (the others being basketball stars David Thompson, 1973 and 1975, and Phil Ford, 1977–78).

The first crouching start in track history. It began with this race at Yale on May 12, 1888. The crouching runner, Charles H. Sherrill, won the race, a 100-yard dash. The other runners (left to right) from Columbia, Princeton and Harvard, have assumed the traditional starting positions. (Courtesy of Yale University Press.)

Jesse Owens as a collegian at Ohio State set or tied 6 world records in one day in 1935, and then won 4 gold medals in the 1936 Olympics, medals he is showing here. Behind him are photos of other events and trophies he has won.

## WRESTLING

### Best Wrestling Teams

Oklahoma State has won 27 N.C.A.A. team wrestling titles, which is more than all the other schools combined. The Cowboys also have had

99 individual winners, almost twice as many as its state rival, Oklahoma (51).

**Fastest Pin**

Don Brown, a 177-pound senior from the University of Oregon, broke a 52-year-old National Collegiate tournament record on March 13, 1980, when he pinned Jay Greiner of Ohio State in only 16 seconds. The previous record, set in 1928, was 19 seconds.

The Rev. Theodore M. Hesburgh, the president of Notre Dame, believes that university presidents have to make sure sports do not overshadow the other aspects of their institutions. He told a banquet audience, honoring the Notre Dame football squad in South Bend, that the job security of coaches and athletic directors should not hinge on a winning season. Father Hesburgh said, "Athletic directors and coaches who support an honest program should have equal support from the university president. Their position and tenure should not be at the mercy of last week's score or the vagaries of a single season. They should never have to worry about being blindsided by those who appoint them."

# INDEX

activism, early, on campus, 32, 33
Agassiz, Louis, 25
  *see also* Harvard; Stanford U.
Air Force Academy, 120
Alabama U., 31, 63, 110, 116, 117, 125
alcoholic beverages, use of, on campus, 63
"Alferd Packer Grill," 37
  *see also* Colorado, U. of
Alfred U., 8
  *see also* Oldest Bells
Alliance College, 135
alligators, 18
  *see also* Southwestern Louisiana
alumnae association, first, 61
  *see also* Wesleyan College
American U., 138
Amherst College, 72, 79, 139
Annapolis, U.S. Naval Academy at, 34
Appalachian State, 148
Arizona State U., 54, 127, 140, 141
Arizona, U. of, 49
Arkansas State, 98, 122
Arlin, Steve, 140
Armour, Richard, 31
Army, 101, 109, 114, 120, 122, 137, 146
athletic-leadership combinations, 124
attendance, college, 90
Auburn U., 49, 98, 102

Babson College, 15
Ball State U., 140
Bando, Sal, 140
Barnard College, 32, 61, 75, 129
bartering for tuition costs, 62, 63
Bartending School of Mixology, 7
  *see also* unusual schools
Bartlett, John, 66, 75
Barton, Laura, 35
  *see also* "streakers"
baseball, college, 139-141
basketball, college, 129-139
Bates, Katherine Lee, 34
Baylor U., 107, 123
Beethoven, death mask of, 31
  *see also* Princeton U.
Benchley, Robert, 42
Bennington College, 56, 83
Benson, Catherine Brewer, 69
Bergen, Edgar, 28
Bernstein, Carl, 30
Bhutan, kingdom of, 10
bicycling, college, 139
Bigelow, Erastus B., 62
bike riding, 85
  *see also* U. of Cal. at Santa Barbara
Birmingham Southern College, 130
black colleges, 25
  *see also* Howard U.
Blair, James, 70
Bogart, Humphrey, 31
Boone, Pat, 32, 33
Boston College, 35, 36, 145, 146
Boston U., 145
Bowdoin College, 72, 128
bowl games, football (extinct), 109, 110, winningest teams in, 110, best streak in, 110, highest score in, 110
Bridgeport U., 148
Brigham Young U., 49, 52, 123
Broderick award winners, 126-128

Bronx Community College Hall of Fame, 26
Brown, Helen Gurley, 30
Brown, Jim, 105
Brown, Nicholas, 73
Brown U., 56, 73, 80, 89, 102, 139
Brumfield, Terry, 140
Bryant, Paul ("Bear"), 116
  *see also* Alabama, U. of
Bryn Mawr College, 26, 32, 61, 67, 75
Buchwald, Art, 42
Bucknell U., 109, 130
Buckley, F. Reid, 11
Buckley, William F., 11, 69
Buena Vista College, 91
Buffalo, U. of, 114

California State U. at Chico, 128
California State U. at Long Beach, 137
California State U. at Northridge, 127, 128
California, U. of, at Berkeley, 53, 55, 63, 67, student revolt, 68
California, U. of, at Irvine, 89, 133, 137
California, U. of, at Los Angeles, 53, 148
  *see also* U.C.L.A.
California, U. of, at San Diego, 40, 53, 75
California, U. of, at Santa Barbara, 85, 139
Cambridge College, 58
  *see also* Harvard
campus housing, 22, 23
Carleton College, 35, 52
Carlisle College, 100
Carlson, Richard, 30
Carroll College, 38, 80
Carter, James Earl, 34
Carthage College, 63
Catawba College, 109
Cedarville College, 117
celebrities, college careers of, 26, 27, 28, 29
Central Michigan State, 98
Centre College of Kentucky, 110
Cerf, Bennett, 42
Charleston, College of, 14
cheap schools, 86
cheerleaders, top 20, 49
"Chicago 7," 28
  *see also* infamous and educated
Chicago, U. of, 36, 50, 99, 104, 114
children on campus, 79
Cincinnati, U. of, 30
Citadel, the, 111
City College of New York, 63, 90
Clarion State, 127
Clark, Dick, 30
Clarke, Dr. Edward Hammond, 77
"Class the Stars Fell On" (West Point, 1913-14), 124
Clemson U., 98, 102, 122
clubs, college, 13
co-ed, first college to begin, 62
  *see also* Cornell U.
Coleman, Jack, 16
Colgate U., 122
college dropouts, famous, 30
college attendance, famous people who didn't make it, 29
College of Comedy, 8
  *see also* unusual schools

College of New Jersey, 68, 74
  *see also* Princeton U.
College of Rhode Island, 68
  *see also* Brown U.
Colman, Ronald, 32
Colorado State (Fort Collins), 120, 139
Colorado, U. of, 37, 101, 103, 143
Columbia School of Journalism, 62
Columbia U., 33, 42, 50, 53, 61, 62, 73, 90, 110, 137, 141, 154
comic journals, college published, 42
Conway, Jill Ker, 79
Coppola, Francis Ford, 34
  *see also* U.C.L.A.
Cornell U., 45, 52, 61, 62, 69, 79, 81, 124, 145, 146
"crawfish boil," world's largest, at U. of Southwestern Louisiana, 18
cross-country, college, 141
Cumberland College, 114
cummings, e.e., 32
Curtis Institute (of Music), 72

dancing on campus, 80, 83
  *see also* Vassar; Smith
Dartmouth College, 30, 68, 71, 75, 77, 124, 146
Davis, Rennie, 28
Dellinger, David, 28
Delta State U., 126
Delaware State, 102, 116, 127
demonstration, most tragic, 61
  *see also* Kent State U.
Denver, U. of, 146
Detroit, U. of, 123
Dishy, Bob, 30
Douglass College, 82
Drake U., 98, 129
Duke U. Medical Center, 95, 122
drinking on campus, 67

Eastern Michigan U., 98
Eastern Washington U., 133
Eastman School of Music at the U. of Rochester, 72
educational television, 25
Eisenhower, Dwight D., 33
  *see also* West Point; Columbia U.
Eliot, Charles William, 63
Elmira College, 38, 61, 82
endowments, schools with the largest, 53, odd, 59
engineering school, largest in U.S., 50
  *see also* Rensselaer Institute
enrollment facts
  demographic breakdown, 93
  facts on student attitudes, 93, 96
Eureka College, 101, 121
expensive schools, most, 56

faculty-student ratio, best, 55
Falk, Peter, 30
"Familiar Quotations, Book of," 75
female applicant, first, 59
Female Medical College of Pennsylvania, 61
fencing, 141
first college in America, 59
Fisk U. Singers, 25
Fitzgerald, F. Scott, 26, 30
"flashers," 87
Flipper, Henry O., 72
Florence State, 130
Florida Southern U., 139

157

## Index (continued)

Florida State, 98, 125
Florida, U. of, 35, 123, 128
Fonda, Jane, 29
football, college, facts, 97-123
Fordham U., 121
Fort Valley State College, 116
Francis, Bevo, 134
Francis Marion College, 132, 133
Franklin, Benjamin, 74
 *see also* Pennsylvania, U. of
fraternities, 13, 63
"Fresh Fruit Magazine," 89
Fresno State, 98
Friedman, Dr. Harvey, 20
Friends World College, 8
frisbees, 17
Froines, John, 28
Furman U., 127, 138, 139
Futter, Ellen, 20
future of college grads, 95

Gable, Clark, 31
Gallup poll, 11
Gehrig, Lou, 141
George Washington U., 148
Georgia Female College, 61
Georgia Tech, 102, 114, 137
Georgia, U. of, 64, 98, 121
Giovanni, Nicki, 31
Glassboro State, 99
globe, world's largest, 15
 *see also* Babson College
goldfish swallowing, 35, 36
golf, 142
 *see also* Ohio State; Wake Forest
Grambling State U., 103
Green, Gerald, 42
gymnastics, 144, 145

Halaby, Lisa, 32
Hampton U., 74
Hampden-Sydney College, 14
Hampshire College, 56
handicapped students, 54
Harris-Stowe State College (St. Louis), 55
"Harvard Law Review," 79
Harvard U., 30, 35, 40, 42, 47, 53, 55, 56, 59, 63, 66, 67, 70, 72, 75, 90, 91, 97, 106, 120, 121, 145, 146, 151, 154
 brief history of, 64, 65
Hasty Pudding Club, 33
Hawaii, U. of, 111, 120
Hawaii, U. of, at Hilo, 135
Hayden, Tom, 28
"hazing," 91
Hearst, William Randolph, expulsion from Harvard, 40
Heisman trophy, 112
Henie, Sonja, 30
Hepburn, Katharine, 26
Herpes research, 51
 *see also* Washington, U. of
Hesburgh, Rev. Theodore M., 156
 *see also* Notre Dame U.
Hildebrand, Dr. Joel, 20
Hillsdale College, 135
hockey, 145, 146
Hoffman, Abbie, 28
Hollins College, 14
Holy Cross U., 123
Hoover, Herbert, 27
Hope College, 40, 41
Houston, U. of, 115, 123, 130, 143
Howard, Gen. Oliver Otis, 71
Howard U., 70

Illinois, U. of, 49, 55, 79, 94, 123, 144
Indiana State U., 49, 114, 137
Indiana, U. of, 77, 86, 101
infamous and educated, 28
Iowa State, 61
Iowa, U. of, 49

Jabbar, Kareem-Abdul, 131
Jackson, Reggie, 140
Jacksonville State, 140

Jacksonville, U. of, 139
James, Jesse, 20
Jefferson, Thomas, 33
 *see also* William and Mary College
Jewell, William, College, 38
Jewish university, America's oldest and largest, 52
 *see also* Yeshiva U.
job problems of graduates, 87
Johns Hopkins U., 146, 147
Johnson, Lyndon Baines, 34
 *see also* Texas State Teacher's College
Juilliard School of Music, 72

Kansas, U. of, 7, 49, 97
Kelly, Nancy, 31
Kent State U., 61, 63, 87
Kentucky State, 130, 133, 137
Kentucky, U. of, at Bowling Green, 89, 117, 125, 130, 137
"Killer" (campus game), 84
 *see also* Michigan, Pennsylvania
King's College, 68
 *see also* Columbia U.
Kinsey, Alfred, 77
Kitts Peak National Observatory, 16
Knoxville College, 116
Koppel, Ted, 30
Kutztown State Teachers College, 36

Lab-For-Germ-Free-Life at Notre Dame, 7
lacrosse, 146
Lafayette U., 106
Lagniappe Day, 18
Lake Superior State College, 42
Land, Edwin, 30
Lane College (Chicago), 115
Langella, Frank, 30
largest school, 56
 *see also* U. of Minnesota
La Salle U., 139
Lee, Gen. Robert E., 26
Leonard, Sheldon, 30
Lewis, Sinclair, 33
libraries, largest college, 52
Library of Congress, 65
Library, New York Public, 65
Lincoln Memorial U., 70, 71
Lippmann, Walter, 32
Livermore Laboratory, 93
Long Island U., 137
Louisiana State, 98, 101, 112, 135, 138, 139
Louisiana Tech, 98, 103
Louisville, U. of, 133, 137
Louvre, the, 17
Ludden, Alan, 34

MacArthur, Gen. Douglas, 28
Mailer, Norman, 31
Maine, U. of, 22
Maravich, Pete, 138, 139
marching band, world's largest college, 38
 *see also* Purdue U.
Mark Twain Summer Institute, 92
Marquette U., 49
Marshall College, 139
Maryland, U. of, 40, 49, 54, 122, 146, 147
mascots, school, 16, 80
Massachusetts Institute of Technology (MIT), 53, 62, 80
Massachusetts Maritime Academy, 117
Massachusetts, U. of, 78
May, Anthony, 18
Medical College of Pennsylvania, 61
medical school for women, first, 61
Medicine and Dentistry, New Jersey College of, 41
Memphis State, 98
Merton, Thomas, 42
Miami-Dade Community College, 54
Miami, U. of (FL), 98, 120, 141
Miami U. (O), 100

Michigan State U., 54, 103, 110, 141
Michigan Tech, 146, 147
Michigan, U. of, 49, 54, 55, 63, 84, 99, 101, 104, 111, 114, 120, 121, 125, 126, 128, 145, 149
Middlebury College (VT), 128
Millay, Edna St. Vincent, 79
Minnesota, U. of, 53, 54, 55, 56, 112, 144, 145, 146
Mississippi State, 98, 122
Mississippi, U. of, 82, 122
Missouri, U. of, 49, 98
MIT (*see* Massachusetts)
Molloy College, 55
Monday, Rick, 140
Monmouth College, 91
Monterey Peninsula College, 120
Moore, Pearl, 132, 133
Morris County College, 151
Morris, Jim, 140
Morrison, Jim, 34
 *see also* U.C.L.A.
Mount Holyoke College, 32, 75, 79, 83
Mount Holyoke Female Seminary, 61
movie actors, former college athletes, 124, 125
Muhlenberg, 109

Nader, Ralph, 32
"National Geographic" magazine, 10
Nebraska, U. of, 109, 111
Nevada, U. of, at Las Vegas, 135
Nevada, U. of, at Reno, 31
Newberry College, 135, 138
Newton, Sir Isaac, death mask of, 31
 *see also* Princeton U.
Newtowne College, 58
 *see also* Harvard
New Mexico State U., 123
New York Fashion Institute of Technology, 55
New York U., 142, 150
North Carolina Agricultural & Technical College, 67
North Carolina State U., 126, 128, 137, 154
North Carolina, U. of, 101, 137
North Dakota, U. of, 63, 80
Northeast Louisiana U., 39
Northeastern U., 54
Northern Colorado College, 115
Northern Illinois, 102, 128
Northern Kentucky State College, 87
northernmost college in the world, Iñupiat U., 21
North Park College (Chicago), 116
North Texas Horseshoeing Institute, 7
 *see also* Unusual Schools
Northwestern College, 112
Northwestern U., famous students from, 28
Notre Dame, 7, 49, 100, 101, 102, 108, 109, 110, 120, 137, 140, 156
Nyad, Diana, 28

Oates, Joyce Carol, 31
Oberlin College, 61, 80, 102
Oglethorpe College, 7
Ohio Central College, 33
Ohio State U., 42, 49, 50, 54, 88, 101, 102, 109, 120, 126, 135, 137, 140, 143, 149, 153, 155
Ohio, U. of, 102, 128
Oklahoma City U., 133
Oklahoma State, 104, 108, 112, 117, 120, 126, 130, 140, 155, 156
Old Dominion U., 126, 128
O'Neill, Eugene, 28
Oregon State, 129, 139
Oregon, U. of, 49, 81, 141, 153, 154, 156
Our Lady of Holy Cross College (New Orleans), 55
Owens, Jesse, 155
 *see also* Ohio State

158

## Index (continued)

Pacific, U. of the, 98, 99, 120, 133
party, world's longest college, 38
  see also San Francisco State College
Penn State, 49, 97, 104, 122, 127, 128, 144, 145
Pennsylvania, U. of, 56, 74, 84, 102, 106, 120
personnel, outstanding college, 20
phonograph records, eating of, 36
  see also U. of Chicago
"Phi Beta Kappa," 70, 124
  see also William and Mary College
Pittsburgh, U. of, 49, 102, 122
Pleshette, Suzanne, 30
poll, college football, 108–109
Ponti, Carlo, 84
Portland State College, 116
Portland State U., 117, 123
pranks on campus, 35–45
pregnancy among students, 79
Princeton U., 26, 31, 32, 42, 45, 53, 56, 68, 74, 97, 98, 154
prison, college in, 20, 21
Pulitzer, Joseph, 62
  see also Columbia School of Journalism
Pulitzer prize winners, 79
Purdue U., 38, 50, 51, 101, 114, 124

Queen's College, 68
  see also Rutgers U.

Radcliffe, 32, 55, 61, 65, 75, 83
Randolph, Harrison (President), 14
Reinhardt, Ad, 42
religion at colleges, 67, 68
Rensselaer Polytechnic Institute, 50
research expenditures, 53
Reutter, Ms. Rita, 20
revenue, college, 53
Reynolds, Bob, 111
Rhode Island, U. of, 123
Rice U., 102, 123
Rio Grande College, 134, 135
rising cost of education, 91
Robinson, Jackie, 118
Rock on Campus, 28
Rollins College, 128
ROTC program, 56
rowing, 146
Rubin, Jerry, 28
Rutgers Female College, 82
Rutgers U., 97, 139

Sabin, Dr. Albert, 30
  see also U. of Cincinnati
Sagan, Carl, 29
  see also Cornell U.
St. Bonaventure, 133
St. Cloud State U., 36, 76, 113
St. John's College, 15
St. Joseph's College, 135
St. Louis U., 148
St. Mary's College, 112, 123
St. Olaf's College, 52
St. Viator College, 115
St. Vincent College, 90
San Diego State, 98, 123
San Francisco State College, 38, 137
San Jose State U., 112, 128
Santayana, George, 42
Sarah Lawrence, 83
school for blacks, first, 70
  see also Howard U.
Selvy, Frank, 138, 139
Seton Hall College, 137
"Seven Sisters," 32, 75
  famous alumnae, 32

sexual attitudes in colleges today, 77–83
Silverman, Fred, 30
Simpson, O. J., 106
Skidmore College, 83
skiing, 146
slingshot, world's largest, 38
  see also William Jewell College
Smith College, 61, 75, 78, 79, 82, 83
smoking in college, 67
soccer, 148
Solomon, Lucy Maynard, 17
Southeastern Louisiana State, 140
Southern California, U. of, 104, 105, 106, 109, 111, 112, 120, 125, 126, 128, 145, 151, 153
Southern Illinois U., 140
Southern Methodist U., 105, 110, 128
South, U. of, silly putty fund, 11
Southwestern Louisiana, U. of, 35
Southwest Missouri State College, 128
Southwestern Missouri State, 128
Southwestern of Tennessee, 135
Spalding College, 91
sports, most intercollegiate, 124
Springfield College, 99, 130
Stafford, William, 31
Stanford U., 26, 53, 56, 67, 91, 110, 111, 116, 128
State U. of New York (SUNY), 50, 57, 73
Stiller, Jerry, 30
Stockton Junior College, 99
"streakers," 35
  see also U. of Florida
students, schools with the most, 54
study time spent by students, 47
suicide rate, campus, 86
Susquehanna U., 99
swimming, 149
Syracuse U., 30, 71, 105, 122, 123, 125

team scoring, highest, 114, 115, 116
Temple U., 129
Tennessee, U. of, 106, 124
tennis, 151
Texas A & M, 43
Texas State Teachers College, 34
Texas, U. of, 34, 51, 128, 142
Texas, U. of, at Austin, 53
Texas, U. of, at El Paso, 9, 10, 39, 41, 53
Texas Women's U., 127, 128
Thorpe, Jim, 126
Thurber, James, 42
Toccoa Falls College, 57
Toledo, 110
track and field, 153
Trenton State, 127
Trinity College, 54
Triton College, 35
trivia, 11
Tucker, Ken, 21
Tufts College, 56
Tulane, 120
Tulsa, U. of, 115, 117, 123
turnaround season, best, 114
Tuskegee Institute, 69
T.V. and FM studio, first college, 71
  see also Syracuse U.
Twain, Mark, study at Elmira College, 23

U.C.L.A., 34, 49, 96, 104, 112, 123, 126, 128, 130, 131, 137, 145, 151, 152
Union College, 63

United States Brewing Academy, 7
  see also unusual schools
unusual schools, 7, 8
U.S.C., see Southern California, U.
U.S. Military Academy, 49
  see also West Point
Utah State, 98, 123, 127, 128, 135

Vallee, Rudy, 31
Vassar College, 32, 60, 61, 73, 75, 78, 79, 82, 83
Vermont, U. of, 128
"veterans of future wars," 45
  see also Princeton U.
Vidal, Gore, 28
Villanova U., 110, 122, 153
Virginia, U. of, 101, 122, 139

Wake Forest U., 49, 139, 143
Waldo, Frank, 33
Walker, Prof. Jearl, 9
Wallace, DeWitt, 30
Washington and Jefferson College, 102
Washington and Lee College, 109, 138
Washington, Booker T., 69
Washington State, 112, 141
Washington, U. of, in Seattle, 51, 69, 108, 112, 123, 153
watermelon toss, 40
  see also Cal., U. of, at San Diego
Waynesburg College, 121
Weiner, Lee, 28
Wellesley College, 61, 67, 75, 80
Wesleyan College, 56, 69
West Chester State College, 127, 128, 148
West Point, 115, 120, 121, 124
Western Carolina U., 133
Western College of Auctioneering, 7
  see also unusual schools
Western Michigan U., 38, 123
Western State, 112, 113
West Liberty State, 117, 118
Westminster College, 82
West Texas State, 110
West Virginia, U. of, 114
"Whiffenpoof Song," 70
  see also Yale U.
White, George L., 25
Whittier College, 121
Wichita State, 102
Widener College, 103, 108
Wilkinson, Bud, 108
William and Mary, 59, 63, 70, 98, 101, 139
Williams College, 91, 109
Williams, Vera, 20
Williams, William D., 17
Wilson, C. Kemmons, 30
Wilson, Edmund, 33
Wilson, Woodrow, 27
Winthrop U., 136
Wisconsin, University of, 11, 53, 54, 125, 128
Wittenberg U., 108
Wolf, Dr. Merrill Kenneth, 17
woman graduate, first, 69
  see also Wesleyan College
women, colleges for, first, 60, 61
Wouk, Herman, 42
wrestling, 154

Yale U., 33, 37, 42, 53, 55, 56, 59, 64, 67, 70, 71, 73, 77, 79, 80, 90, 98, 107, 120, 125, 142, 146, 154; "God and Man at Yale," 69
Yeshiva U., 52
youngest undergraduate, 17

159